REFLECTIONS:
A Collection of Short Stories

EL Walker

This book is dedicated

In loving memory

Of my father, Jimmy Walker Jr

And to

My mom, my family, friends

Thank you for supporting me on

This journey.

Constantly In Motion

Chapter 1

The first time I saw Camille, I thought that she was breathtaking. And like a breath of fresh air into my lungs. She was what you considered the popular girl in high school, guys wanted a piece of her in every way that you could imagine; girls wanted her in the same way. I wanted her too, but not just to have sex with her and brag to my friends about what I did. But to be with her, and treat her in away that she has never been treated. I've seen guys brag about dating her and getting some action on the first night. All I could do was shake my head because they were talking about her like she was a bitch and plus she liked girls anyway. Now when it comes to me, I knew that I wasn't her type. She was in an elite squad of people and I was just in a squad. I wore a uniform every Monday, I was apart of different teams and had a huge family. Because when you are in Army JROTC, that's what you do and that's what you have.

One night after a football game, I made my way to the front of the school to wait for my cousin to pick me up. Everyone was practically gone. I spotted Camille standing there alone, she looked a bit upset. But I couldn't help but to wonder why she was still here and not gone with her friends. After receiving a text from my cousin, I decided to go and talk to her. "Excuse me, Camille?" "Do I know you?" "no, my name is Noelle, and I just wanted to know if you could use a ride," "I don't know you like that," "I know, but its late and you're here alone, I just figured you could use a lift," "I'm fine thank you." She moved a few feet away, I turned around and started to head towards my cousin's car. Then I stopped, I turned back around, "believe it or not but we have been going to the same school since elementary, I know you because you are the most popular girl in school and people would kill to be your friend. Now I know we just met, and I know that I am not your

BFF. But I couldn't live with myself knowing that you are out here in the dark alone. And to top it off, what if something were to happen to you and I was the last one to see you," "I know that you mean well, but you don't owe me any favors," "let me put it to you like this, you can either stay here and wait another hour for your ride or you can come with me and get dropped off. If you don't feel like going home then you can come with us to my birthday party. Now what do you want to do?" I took a deep breath and stood there waiting for an answer, "I don't feel like going home," "then lets go." I walked over to where she was standing and picked up her gym bag. We both walked to the car and got inside.

At the party, I introduced Camille to everyone at the table and then I pointed to a corner where my parents were sitting. As we sat down, we all ordered food to eat and then goofed off as we waited for it to come. My bestfriend, Rose, got up from the table and waved for me to follow her. I went outside with her, "whats up with Camille?" "No clue, she was standing there alone and I talked to her," "you better use this time to your advantage because you may never get a chance like this again." We made our way back inside and sat down to eat.

When the party was over, we drove Camille to her house; we waited to make sure that she got inside safely. She kept knocking on the door and calling but no one answered. She came and got back in the car, I took a look at her and she looked like she just wanted to break down and cry. My cousin drove us to my place. We got out of the car; I pulled her bag out the back and walked her inside the house. I sat her bag down in the guest room, "there is a bathroom right there, so feel free to use it and I have some sweats that you can borrow," "ok." I left the room and went into mine. I sat on my bed wiping my hands across my face, then I got undressed and took a quick shower.

I went back downstairs and knocked on the guest bedroom door, "if your still up I'm in the living room watching TV if you want to join me and the clothes are by the door." I walked away, made my way into the kitchen, I pulled out the brownies that I had made last night and poured two glasses of milk. I made my way into the living room, sat everything on the table, sat down and started watching *The Brothers*. "Hey," Camille said as she sat down on the couch, "hi," I ate my brownie, "I've never seen this movie before," "it's funny; I think you'll like it." I pushed the glass of milk toward her and the plate of brownies. Within ten minutes she was laughing, eating, and drinking.

Once the movie was over, I took the plate and glasses into the kitchen. "Can I ask you something?" "Anything," "where are your parents?" "Oh there away on a weekend get away, they do it twice a month and leave me and my brother here," "where is your brother?" "at his friend's house, I let him sleep over and hangout with his friends," "you're a sweet sister," "I try, plus he gets on my nerves sometimes," we both smiled. "What about your folks?" "My dad is a cool guy I guess, he has a drinking problem and my mom tries to keep the family together," "I would say I'm sorry to hear that, but it looks like you hear it enough," "I do." We both made our way to our bedrooms, "Noelle," I stopped on the steps, "I had a good time tonight, maybe we could do it again sometime," "sounds good to me, just let me know when," "ok," "goodnight Camille," "goodnight Noelle." I walked into the room, closed my door and got in the bed. This was how I met the future love of my life.

Chapter 2
2 years later

I and Camille have been together for two years now, it was amazing how one night could change your life forever. It was something that you would see in a movie, just watching love bloom like a flower right before your eyes. I love this girl, I am in love with this girl and she feels the same way back.

I would sit in the chair, while she chilled on the couch studying. She wanted to be a psychologist and I wanted to be an EMT at the paramedic level. I was learning anatomy, which I and Camille would go over sometimes. And I was learning about physiology. The one thing that I had to my advantage was that when I was fifteen years old my cousin would let me follow her in the hospital and she would teach me first hand about how to do stitches, EKGs, almost anything and everything that I needed to know. The chief even allowed me to do a ride along because this was going to be the future hospital that I was going to be working at once I got done with school.

"Hey, if you do my math I will do your anatomy," said Rose standing in the doorway, "I like doing my anatomy," I smiled and looked over at Camille, "I didn't need to know that," we all started laughing, "it helps me learn better and I remember better," "I bet." We all took a break from studying and started to watch TV. "I have an early class tomorrow, I'm going to get some sleep," Camille kissed me, "I will put your books together," "thanks baby, goodnight Rose." She walked out of the room looking like she wanted to fall over. I got up stacked and closed her books, put all her papers in her backpack and placed it by the door. Eventually, I went up to the bedroom and got into bed with her. I watched her sleep peacefully for a few seconds, and then I kissed her on her forehead, and then turned on my side. As I slowly drifted off to sleep I felt her arm go around me and her body close to me.

The next day, I felt like it was going to be a boring day, sitting in class, listening to the professor talk. That quickly changed once a friend of mine called me up and asked if I wanted to ride in the ambulance with him today. I quickly said yes, got dressed in my paramedic uniform and an hour later he picked me up. "I know you've been wanting to do this for a min," said Chris "hell yeah, I couldn't wait," "why do you want to be an EMT?" "I was born to save lives," "that's what everyone says," "honestly, I have always loved to help people and there are times where I would put others before myself. So being an EMT is the ultimate job for me," "I feel you on that."

We sat down at the local Starbuck's eating some oatmeal and drinking some tea. I wasn't that much of a Starbuck's person but I do love there oatmeal. "You ready for this?" "What?" "We just got a call, there has been a shooting at Martin Luther King Jr. Middle School, and are you ready?" "Yes, let's roll." We started speeding down the street as our siren made people get out the way. I felt my adrenaline reach an all time high. Once we got to the school, there were police and fire trucks all over the place. Everyone was pulling us left and right, "call me if you need me Noelle." I started helping some of the children who were on the ground; some of them only had minor bruises, some needed to be rushed to the ER. "Excuse me, I need your help," said a female teacher, "sure," "he's been shot, one of the students said that he saved her," "what's his name?" "Brian." I saw him laying there on the ground, I started to try and stop the bleeding, I yelled at the teacher to go and get some more help. I lifted his head up, and placed pressure on his wounds, "you can't talk," blood slowly started to come out of his mouth, "is she ok?" "Yea, she's fine, you saved her," "I wasn't thinking," "you did what you thought was right," I looked around and yelled, "I need help over here." More blood started to come out of him, "I'm going to die," "Brian, you are not going to die, not like this," "tell my parents...tell them I love them...tell them I am sorry...and I," he grabbed my hand and held it tight, "I...I love you too." I shook him a few times, "Brian," I started doing CPR, "Brian wake up." Footsteps ran toward me, "he's gone Noelle, he's gone." On the ride back home, I sat there playing it over and over again in my head, "we can't save them all," Chris said.

Back at home, I sat on the floor in the den, crying. My uniform soaked in blood, Rose and Camille sat there with me, just waiting for words to come out of my mouth. But all I could say was "I couldn't save him." They both held me, "you don't understand," they looked at me, "that was the first patient that died in my arms, it was Brian," "What?" yelled Camille, "my first patient that I had, that died in my arms was Brian, my baby brother…this is his blood…I couldn't save him." I placed my hand over my eyes and cried.

Camille had finally got me to get up and out of my clothes, while Rose called my parents. When they had got home we embraced each other, I kept sayin that I was sorry. And all I heard was that it wasn't my fault over and over again.

Four days later…we buried my brother. Part of me wanted to quit, but I couldn't because saving lives is what I want to do. I know now that I can't save them all, whether it's a stranger or family. The pain will always be the same.

Chapter 3
Four years later

    I quietly sat down on the stairs listening to the conversation that Camille was having with her friends. I know that it is wrong to ease drop, but I couldn't help myself. Camille didn't always tell me how she felt about certain things, and other times I wouldn't ask because I had a fear of being rejected or getting into a big pointless argument about it. Plus our fifth year anniversary was coming up and I was hoping to get a hint. "Noelle doesn't want that," I heard one of her friends say, "y'all have been together for four years and she has yet to buy you a ring," "we can't get married anyway and it will be five years in three months," "it doesn't matter, you could have a ceremony," "just seems like to much," "Camille you two have been together since you were sixteen and now you're twenty-two, nothing has went wrong and nothing will. Just talk to her about it." I quickly got up and walked back into the bedroom, "baby, I will be back," I heard Camille yell, "ok love."

    At this point I knew that it was time to talk to Rose, because two years ago she had said Camille is going to want a little more after awhile. I just didn't want to believe it. Not everyone goes into a relationship thinking this is going to last a lifetime; you just go into it day by day. Until one day you look up and you've been dating for five years. And the funny part is, is that it doesn't even feel like it.

    Me and Rose met up for lunch at Taco Bell, she truly loved this place. "You know this isn't real Mexican food," I said sitting down at the table, "yes it is," "no its not, this is Americas definition of Mexican food," "it's real Mexican," "oh yea, then go to an authentic Mexican place to eat and then you tell me if it's the same," "whatever." Rose went to grab the food when our number was called. She sat back down at the table and placed the food out. "So let me guess," I turned and looked at her, "you over heard a convo that you weren't supposed to hear and what I said a few years ago is now comin to light," she smiled at me then took a bite of her taco. "I don't even think that she will talk to me about it...she can talk to everyone else but me," "then bring it up to her, I have three months until it is officially five years. What are you going to do?" "I was planning on working, and then..." "What? I know that look," "I've been thinking about joining the Army," "shut the fuck up," she said in a surprised voice. I wiped my hand across my face, "it will be the reserve so I won't be gone all the time," "if this is something that you feel in your heart is right than I am behind you 100%."

Camille was at home when I got there, she seemed to be a bit upset so I knew that I had to tread lightly. "Whats wrong?" she stood up and looked at me, "what the fuck is this?" she screamed at me as she threw my Army information on the bed, "I hope you have a damn good explanation for this," "I am considering joining the Army Reserve, I can have my education paid for and build a better future for us," "by leaving me? That doesn't make anything better," "what happened to you being the woman that would always support me in whatever I do," "this is just crazy." She brushed passed me and walked out the door. There was only so much that could be done when she was upset, it was because we are always around each other and yet we can still manage to have a relationship with our friends outside of us.

I got into bed and just laid there, I didn't know wat was going to happen next. I just hoped that it would be good. I turned on to my side, closed my and slowly went to sleep. I felt her arm go round me and her breathing on my neck. "I'm sorry for walking out on you like that, if this is something that you want to do then I am going to be with you every step of the way," she gently kissed the back of my neck. I turned around to face her, my hand resting on the side of her face, I moved my thumb across her lips, I pulled her in to kiss me. I started to kiss and suck on her neck, "you tryin to start something baby," "no I'm not," I bit her on her neck, knowing that's what she likes. Hearing her lightly moan in my ear as my hand moved between her legs, she gets on top of me, removes her shirt and bra. "I could always stop," "shut up and fuck me how I like it baby." And that is exactly what I did.

The next day I found myself at Jared with Rose looking at rings for Camille. This shit was so frustrating, everyone looked better then the next, the next looked better then the other, and each one seemed so perfect for her. I felt like the woman behind the counter was becoming impatient with me. I think Rose sensed my irritation, told the lady that we will be back in an hour and we left the store. "Fuck man, you would think that the hardest part is asking," "calm down, you know that whatever you get her she is going to love it," "I know but I just want it to be perfect because the first time is always the best time," "true," "let's go to the bank and get myself a ring," "lets do it."

Three weeks, it's already been three weeks since I bought the ring and she still doesn't have it on her finger. There were so many ways that I could give it to her, that it was hard for me to pick. All I really could do was lay across the bed twirling the ring in my hand. Time is not on my side right now, there has to be a way for me to do this. I quickly closed the ring up in my hand as Camille walked into the room, "what was that?" "What was what?" "That in your hand," "it's nothing," "are you lying to me?" "Yep." I got off the bed, kissed her gently on her lips and then walked out the room.

I sat in the living room reading my anatomy book; I liked to stay current with everything that was going on so that I could perfect my skill. "Hey Baby," I looked up at Camille and her friends walking into the room, "hey," she sat down on my lap and stole a few kisses, "I'll let you girls have the room," I moved Camille off of me and got up. "You know you don't have to leave," "it's cool baby," "for the past few weeks, everytime I walk into the house you leave or act funny," "I just have a lot on my mind that's all," "and you can't even talk to me about it," "it's not that…its just that it involves you, and I can't talk about certain things dealing with you to you," "Noelle, you can talk to me about anything," "not this," I kissed her on her forehead and turned to walk out the room, "Noelle," "I love you." I continued to walk and then stopped when I heard her friend say, "if she loves you so much then why doesn't she put a ring on your finger," I walked back into the room, "why can't you mind your own damn business?" "Camille is my business," "you are a childhood friend, not her cousin, her sister or anything else for that matter, and what is between us, stays between us," "then just answer me this,

14

why haven't you put a ring on her finger? If you give her everything else that she wants why can't you give that to her?" I rubbed the back of my neck, put my hand in my pocket, and held the ring in my hand, "you see you can't even give me an answer," "Terri just stop it," said Camille, "Naw baby, I can handle this…I just wanted to talk to you about this in private, but sense your friends believe that they are entitled to everything going on in our relationship, and you are going to tell them anyway, let's put it out in the open," "what are you talking about baby?" "I know that you don't want to do anything that I am not ready for, and everyone on this planet knows that I would give you the world if I could. I love you more then anything; you are my life, my heart, and more then just my everything. And when I hear about the whole ring thing, I panic because I feel like we are better how we are and that the marriage will complicate things," "Noelle, nothing will ever change between us our love is to strong for that…I know that we have had our ups and downs, going back and forth but this is going to work, whether I am your wife or just your girlfriend," "and that's the thing, I want you to be my wife," I looked up at her, "I want you to be my wife, I can't imagine my life without you at this point," "so what are you saying?" I pulled the ring out of my pocket, and held it out for her to see, "I want you to marry me…so Camille Shaw, will you marry me?" I felt myself stop breathing for that whole moment, "yes," I placed the ring on her finger and we hugged and kissed.

Three months later…all of our friends and family set in the glass room that we had reserved for our ceremony, it was amazing to see that it was raining, Camille loved the rain and it seemed to fit on this very day. I stood at the altar with Rose by my side; we started whispering to each other, "dude, you know my girl is going to start asking for this shit soon," "it might be good for you," "why you say that?" "Because you got to many bitches on the side and a good girl on your arm, and this might actually make you focus," "you know me so well," "don't let your past control your future Rose," I looked at her, "you're better then that." The music started to play as Camille made her way down the aisle, it started to rain harder with each step that she took, once she reached me, the rain had lighten up and you could see a rainbow behind us. We sealed the love that we have for each other, and I wouldn't have it any other way. Camille is now my wife and I am hers, forever and always.

Chapter 4
Two years later

"Wake up sleepy head," I felt Camille's hand on the back of my neck. I sat up as I opened my eyes. "You should really get into bed sometimes," "I couldn't really sleep, so I just studied for a little bit," "and watched episodes of Nurse Jackie and Grey's Anatomy," "that too," "I have to get goin." She moved her hand threw my hair, leaned my head back and kissed me. I kept kissing her, "baby I have to go," "just one more," "your one more goes into something more," we kissed a few more times, "you can have me when I get home." I laid my head back down as I watched her walk away. *Two years we had been married already and it has also been two years since I joined the Army Reserve.* We have also been working on starting a family of our own, even though the thought of me being a good mother scares the shit out of me.

All I wanted to do was throw my phone across the room when it started ringing, "hello," I said in my best awake voice, "you ready? I'm outside," "be out in 20." I hung up the phone, showered, got dressed, and then made my way outside. "How can you be so awake after pulling a double?" "I am used to it, you will be soon as well." I yawned as I got into the ambulance and went to work.

Falling into the pillows on the bed was the best feeling I have ever got after getting home from work. I figured that my body would be used to this by now, I guess I was wrong. I sat up in the bed, took off my work uniform and laid back down in my boxers and sports bra. I felt her lips kiss down my spine, her hands caressing my body, "let's finish what we started baby," she whispered in my ear. She turned me on to my back, pulled off my boxers, and I felt her tongue part the lips of my pussy and taste me, sucking, biting, and licking me up and down. Camille knew how to please me just right, the only girl that I knew who could make me cum multiple times. I pulled her up to my lips, and undressed her as we kissed.

"Good morning ladies," I said walking into the kitchen and kissing Camille on her neck, "hey love, do you work today?" I let out a big yawn, "sure do, but I am sure that I will be home before you," "I am going to go to the doctor's today," "I can meet you up there," "you don't have to do that," I kneeled down next to her, "bur I want too." She placed her hand on the side of my face and I smiled at her…four hours later…I sat next to Camille waiting for her to get an ultra sound, I held her hand as the doctor showed us where the baby was, at seven weeks the baby was doing just fine. I couldn't believe that we were really about to have a baby. And every morning that I wake up I would get to see him or her on the fridge.

"You look a lot better now," said Chris drinking his coffee, "I think I am finally starting to adjust," "about time shit, I thought that I was going to have to get you an energy drink," "I don't like those." We left the coffee shop and got back on the road, then a call came in for a freeway collision, I flipped the switch to turn on the sirens and we started speeding down the street. We arrived to the scene of the accident, you could tell just by looking that it happened because of a big rig, we were all running around trying to find the serious wounded people, tag them and get them on the helicopter on the bus. Me and Chris eventually left the scene to drive a few people up to the hospital, there was so much chaos around us. I really hated when accidents like this happened.

I started helping out with what I could but I had to roll out with Chris to help with more traumas that would be coming in. "Noelle," I heard my name being called as I was making my way out the door, "Terri," I walked over to her, "are you ok?" I started to check her out, "I'm fine, it was so scary," "I have to go, I have to get back out there," "Camille is here, she had to get rushed to the ER," I stopped in my tracks along with my heart, "what room?" "I don't know, they just told me to wait in the waiting room and they would find me," I started running around the hospital trying to find her, I opened the last door and found her, "get out of her Noelle she is in good hands," said my cousin as she operated on her. I paced the room back and forth waiting for my cousin to come out, when she finally entered she took me in to see her.

I stayed there all night and day waiting for her to wake up, it wasn't that comfortable sleeping in these damn chairs though…I woke up with her staring at me, "I didn't want to wake you," "you could of," "you looked comfy," "ha, yea right," "come lay with me," I got into bed with her. "What's wrong?" she looked up at me as I held her in my arms, "you just scared the fuck out of me. I thought I had lost you," "I'm fine baby and so is our child," she kissed me on my lips, "we lost the baby Camille," "what?" "We lost the baby, they tried everything that they could to save her, but we lost her," "it was a girl?" "Yes, it was a girl." I held her tight in my arms as silent tears came out of her eyes. It was hard for me to be strong for her because that pain hit me just as hard, but I knew that it couldn't compare to being the mother who was about to give birth.

Chapter 5

Camille threw herself into work and school, every time I tried to pull her out of it we would get into a big argument. Then there were nights when she wouldn't come home because she would stay at Terri's place. To top it off we barely kissed, hugged, or even had sex. And this had been going on for two weeks now. I wanted her to start to heal and get better, I wanted her to know that it wasn't too late for us to try to have a baby again. It was as if she never wanted me touch her again, but then I started thinking about her past and I realized that this wasn't the first time she had lost a child...*when she was fourteen years old, she was raped by a friend of the family and ended up getting pregnant by him. She wanted to keep the child because she wasn't going to blame it for what happened. Then one night her dad was in his drunken rage and started to argue with her mother. Camille tried to protect her, and he put hands on the both of them which caused her to lose the baby.*

I decided that this had been going on for to long, so when I got home from work, I prepared myself to argue with her. I took a deep breath before I walked in. "Hey Noelle," said Terri looking up at me, "Camille we need to talk and they need to go," "there is nothing that we need to talk about and they are staying because I am studying," "and that's what we need to talk about, your always studying, you always avoid me, and you never have anything to say to me," "I have a lot going on in school right now, I am working on getting my masters," "I thought that when you love someone you make time for them no matter what, and I have all this time for you and all you can say is school...you're not the only one who lost someone, we both lost a child, and the sad thing is, is that we have been together for six years and you still think that you have to handle shit on your own," "Noelle not right now," "then when? When you become numb to it and don't give a fuck anymore, don't you know that everything you do is affecting me," I could tell that she was trying to hold back tears, "I just want my wife back, I want her to know that no matter what happens good or bad, that we could make it together," "I didn't realize I was hurting you this much," "well now you do," I let out a sigh, "go head and study with your friends, I'm sorry for interrupting."

Warm hot water, along with some bubbles filled the bathtub as I started to get undressed. *I can't believe I just went off on her like that, but she needed to know.* I started to soak in the bathtub with a towel over my eyes. This just seemed like a very long day. The bathroom door opened, I took the towel off of my eyes and looked over at Camille. "I should be used to sharing how I feel about certain situations with you by now, I love you and I shouldn't act this way toward you its just that because of everything in my…" "You don't owe me know explanation, your childhood was your life before I entered it. And I am not going to hold it against you." I closed my eyes and turned back around, I heard clothes hit the floor, Camille got into the bathtub with me. "I thought you had to study with your girls," "I'm making time to be with my wife." Her tongue slid into my mouth as we shared a long passionate kiss, "I just want you to hold me," Camille said to me as she laid her head on my chest and started crying.

Chapter 6

Things had gotten better between me and Camille after I went off on her. I was never one to raise my voice, because I felt that if my anger got to high I would have an out of body experience. I'm not saying that I would be violent towards people, I am simply saying that I wouldn't feel like myself and hate what I had turned into. When I was younger and I would be sad or upset about things I would grab a rock cd and play the same song over and over again until I felt myself get lifted and feel better. Most might think its crazy, when it comes to the music that I listen too, but I really don't give a fuck what they think because we are all too different to be alike. And I don't know about you, but I love being unique from others because you never know what to expect from me. Even when it came to Camille she would say that I sounded like a white girl, I would laugh and just say I'm educated. I guess if your race is a certain way then that is how people expect you to talk. Its funny to me, because I don't use the word nigga in every sentence that I speak like some people I know or I may not even use that much slang, but that's just me.

Now if you fuck with me the wrong way then I might show you how much of a nigga I can be. We can't control how we are raised, how we speak or what we do in life, all I know is that as long as you stay true to yourself and who you are as a person, then you will be good for the rest of your life. Just take it by the hand and walk with it, otherwise it can cause you pain and so much destruction. But then again, it's all apart of life.

When it comes to me and Camille on the other hand, things were just beginning to scratch the surface.

Chapter 7

      When I got home from work, I got the mail out of the mailbox and made my way into the house. I placed a piece of the mail of the mail on the table so that Camille could see it when she got home. I sat on the patio, watching the clear sky suddenly get cloudy. So many thoughts were racing threw my mind, but I tried to remain calm until I got a chance to talk to Camille about what was about to happen. It started to drizzle a little bit as thunder roared like a lion in the sky and lighting shot out. It was going to rain hard; it would be good for Cali right about now because it had been hot for the past few months. Camille had finally came home and sat down in the chair next to me. "My unit is getting deployed baby," I looked her in the eye, "why are you getting mad?" "because I didn't want you to do this shit in the first place," "I'm just as scared as you are and I cant be thousands of miles away knowing that you're scared as hell and thinking that I am not coming back to you," "my deepest fear is that you are going to come back in a box," "I am always going to come back to you, because I am not done loving you yet," I sat there trying to hide my smile, "you stole that from Grey's Anatomy," I started laughing, "it sounded good though didn't it?" "Yea it did, I love you so much," "I will always love you so much more."

The rain started to come down more, the look of lust entered Camille's eyes, her fantasy was to have sex in the rain. And today was the best moment to make it happen. Camille took the cushions off the chairs and laid them on the ground, she stood there removing each part of her clothes while getting soaked in the rain, she pulled me out of the chair and took off my EMT uniform, we both stood there admiring each others bodies. We started to kiss as we laid down on the cushions kissing, letting the rain hit our bodies, everything I did I took my time, I wanted her to feel me even when I was no longer there. Her pussy was still just as sweet when I tasted it, even though the rain had got there first. Camille was still so wet for me right now and I was the same, I started to make her climax as the thunder became heavier. Feeling her nails in my back, the moans that left her mouth, only wanted me to make this night unforgettable.

The next day, we laid in bed holding each other close. I felt like she didn't want to let me go, the feeling was mutual. I texted rose as I laid in bed with Camille letting her know that I would be getting deployed. "Just come home safe man, you know we are going to hit the bar before you go," "I know man, that's how you operate," "that's only to keep from crying and worrying about you," "I am going to spend a lot of my time with Camille so just come over whenever," "after I get my girl settled into my place I will make my way over there." It surprised me to find out that her girl was moving in with her because Rose is damn near equal to Shane from off The L Word.

I found myself at the bar with Rose, we sat there drinking and having a good time, I would watch her go out on the dance floor and flirt with a few females. I just sat at the bar thinking about getting deployed, wondering how Camille was going to be without me there, and wondering how I was going to be without her with me. I knew that we were about to communicate with each other a lot better. I just wanted to come back to her in one piece and not in pieces. "Noelle," Rose bumped into me, "dance with me," I sat there looking at her. Don't get me wrong my best friend is sexy as hell, I couldn't lie and say that I wasn't attracted to her, I just knew that we were better off as friends because I knew who she really was underneath.

Chapter 8

A few weeks later I found myself in Iraq with my unit. I couldn't believe that it was so fuckin hot over here. Whenever I got a chance I would call back home and talk to my wifey or best friend. There was only so much that I could reveal about what was going on over here. The main thing I would say was that it was hot as a bitch out here.

When we would go on patrols the kids would come up and talk to us, it was fun talking with the locals and trying to learn there language. I also got a chance to help some of the locals who were in need. This was the best decision that I could of ever made, helping people made me feel like I was making a little difference in the world no matter how big or small.

"SGT Michaels," "over here," I put my hand in the air, I looked up at the soldier standing before me, her eyes were green, brown smooth skin that kind of resembled Rihanna, part of me started to wonder if she spoke with an accent, "how can I help you?" "Well SGT, my arm has been giving me problems lately and I also got cut on my arm when I was helping move wood," "sit down, take off your jacket, and let me take a look at you Specialist." I put on some gloves and started to check out her arm, while doing so I was talking to her at the same time, and then without warning I popped her arm back into place. She looked up at me and I smiled as I started to clean her wound and get her back out there.

"Hey Noelle we're about to go play some football, you might want to be out there when I bust some of these fools in they face," said SGT Spade, he was a hard ass, thinking that he was the shit in anything and everything that he did," "y'all are really about to play football," "yea girl do you want in?" "Fuck it lets do it." We started playing a smooth game of football, I was the quarterback, I kept throwing good hits to my team mates, and then one member of the other team started to get irritated. "Damn it Spade you're cheating," "stop being a bitch and play the game," I hiked the ball and threw another pass to him, I watched as he was tackled to the ground by the shit talking soldier. I couldn't believe we had just started playing and a fight had broken out.

"You have quite an arm," said the Specialist walking over to me, "most of my friends are guys and sport junkies as I like to call them," "that's funny, well I'll see you around." I watched as she walked away and I went back to work. "You know she is attracted to you," said Hinson pushing my head to the side," "she has a wifey," said Cooper sitting on the other side of me, "how long have you been together?" "eight years," "that's cool man," I looked over at Cooper, "talking wouldn't hurt though," "Michaels," "Cooper, you know I wouldn't do anything to jeopardize my relationship," "then make sure she knows that." I sat back in my chair as they got up and walked away.

Chapter 9
7 months later

In two weeks I was going to be going back home, I kept telling Camille that I didn't know when and that I should find out soon. You would think that it was wrong for me to do that, but I just wanted to surprise her when she was at school or at Starbucks with all her friends. Spade had came in and told me that we were about to head out; I grabbed my gear and followed him. "I am so fuckin happy to be leaving this place," said Hinson as she was driving, "I'm with you." I started looking out the windows as she drove, "stop the car," I started pointing out the window, "I think it's a person," "bullshit SGT," "pull over," "we have orders," "and I took an oath, so you're either going to stop or I'm jumping out this bitch." Hinson stopped the vehicle and we all got out, I ran over to what I saw, it was a wounded soldier, I quickly checked his pulse and gave him some water, "I am going to check the perimeter," said Spade. The soldier grabbed my arm, "stop them...stop them," he kept saying, and then his heart stopped beating. When I stood up, I felt like I was moving in slow motion, I watched as our other combat vehicles took to the sky, Spade ran back my way and grabbed my shirt, shots started to fire as we ran behind the vehicle for cover...my heart was beating out of my chest because no one knew if we were going to live or die today.

Chapter 10
2 weeks later

I walked out of the airport and greeted Rose, she helped me put my bags in the car and then gave me a big hug afterwards. I knew that I had the kind of vibe that said I didn't want to talk about it, but I knew that after awhile it would come out. It would all come out. I looked at the time and saw that I had four hours before Camille would be meeting up with her friends at Starbucks. I took off my uniform, sat there staring at it, I hope that this blood would come off. I ran a warm bath as I unpacked my bag and put everything away. I walked into the bathroom, got into the bath and I just started crying. After a minute I let myself sink under the water and held my breath for as long as I could, I wasn't trying to kill myself, I just wanted to drown out the noise.

I grabbed my uniform and placed them on the backseat of the car, before I left I made myself a bowl of cereal. There were so many things that I was carving for right now. I made my way to the cleaners to drop off my uniform and then I headed up to where Camille was. I came to a stop so that a mother in her kids could walk across the street. The asshole behind me kept honking his horn and thought it would be a good idea to pass me on the left. The bastard hit the mom and her kids, for a quick second I had a flashback *Iraq the children, the dead children*. I shook it off, jumped out my car, "call 911," I yelled to the bystanders as I walked over to them, "I didn't see them," "what the fuck is your problem, you act like what you have to do is so damn important that you nearly kill a mother and her kids," "I'm sorry," "fuck you and your sorry." Once the ambulance arrived I helped get them on to the back of the bus. *Even though the kids were alive and so was the mother, all I could see were dead bodies*. I called Rose and told her to meet me at the park.

As we sat there, I told her about what had just happened, I told her that the worst thing anyone could see were dead children. "It's going to take some time for you to heal Noelle," "I haven't even been back for twenty-fours and shit is already affecting me," "whatever you need I am right here for you, so are all your friends and your wifey," "it's just gonna be hard," "you can handle anything that comes your way." I smiled as I ate my ice cream and talked with Rose about her girl living with her and now she wants to marry her. "Hey SGT," said the Specialist, "you live in Cali?" "Yea, you didn't see it on my records," "I wasn't paying that much attention and please call me Noelle," "ok Noelle, and you can call me Jena," "this is my best friend Rose," "hi nice to meet you," they shook hands, "I will see you around sometimes," she said smiling as she walked away. I looked up at Rose, "what?" she just shook her had and started smiling.

I chilled at Rose's place until later on tonight because Rose was heading out to Oasis to dance her ass off. We made our way up to Upland, got some food from Del Taco and waited to see her and her friends arrive. "We need to get some Amapolla later on tonight, I want Mexican food," "that shit is to damn hot for me," "you can get tacos or something girl, come on please," "only because you said please and I know that you've been wanting this," we watched as my girl and her crew pulled up, she got out the car looking sexy as hell, I was happy that she was mine and no one else could have her.

Around 9:50pm we walked into the club so that we could still get in for free. It surprised me to see that the club was halfway packed because usually there aren't that many people in here. We stood in the back where we couldn't be seen; I would send Camille her favorite drinks and watched as she searched the crowd for the mystery woman. I told Rose to go over there and talk to her; I waited to get myself together. I took a shot of Patron and then made my way to where she was. In silence I stood behind her, once she turned around she most of kissed me so fast that I couldn't help but to smile inside.

Back at home, Camille stripped down to her bra and panties, she crawled on top of me and started giving me sweet kisses as she lifted up my shirt and pulled it off. Then she removed my jeans, kissed me on my inner thighs, "Camille," "yes love," "I just want to hold you right now," "is everything ok?" "Yes, I just want to hold you and look at you." She laid her body against mine and I put a blanket over us. I didn't go to sleep until three in the morning.

Chapter 11

Slowly, but surely, with each passing day I was getting used to being in civilian life again. Although I did have the occasional nightmares, and those would make me not want to sleep at night. Cooper and Hinson even came down for a visit for a few weeks and that helped even more because we not only experienced the same situation from different view points, but we were able to talk about it with each other and understand it. I still only shared a few things with Camille because she would hold me after I had a nightmare. And saying, "I'm ok," "I'm fine," so often that it just gets tiring. So I shared with her to help her try and understand better. Some things made her laugh, but my nightmares made her cry.

I walked into the bedroom, jumped on the bed, and started watching TV while Camille was taking a shower. I picked up her cell phone and started leaving little notes on various days of her calendar, then I started being goofy and taking pictures of myself with her camera, but a text message interrupted my fun. I didn't mean to read it. I moved it off the screen and sat her phone down as she walked out the bathroom. She picked it up and quickly glanced at me, then started to get dressed.

We went to March Air Force Base to do some grocery shopping, "peach cobbler sounds good," I said to Camille as I started to fill up a bag, "ok love," I put them down in the cart. I ventured away from Camille and started walking around the store, "I'm starting to think that you are stalking me Jena," "I can't help that we shop at the same place," "so I am wondering who do you talk to about Iraq?" "Friends, people who have been there, it makes it easier and some days or even weeks are better then others," "it's just been beaten me down for the past few days now," "here take my number and anytime you need to vent just call me," "thanks." I walked away and went to look for Camille, she was standing in the checkout line, and I stood there with her.

On the ride home Camille looked like she wanted to bite my head off, I knew that she might have saw me talking to Jena so I just decided to get the argument out of the way. "Whats the problem?" "Who was that female you exchanged numbers with?" "We were overseas together, I wanted to know who she talked to about being over there," "I am someone who is qualified in this field, I don't understand why you just can't talk to me," "its not that easy seeing my wifey as my therapist," "whateva," "its not whateva," "it is because you can talk to everyone else but me," "that sounds familiar," I parked the car in the garage as she jumped out and slammed the door behind her as she walked in the house. I quickly followed.

"You want to know about the dead children that we saw, holding weapons up to people, you want me to tell you how I saw bodies blown apart, what the fuck else do you want to know, so that you can understand that this isn't something that is easy to talk about for me," I took a quick breath, walked back into the garage and started to bring the groceries inside and put them away. I washed my hands and started peeling the peaches. "I don't want to argue with you," I turned and faced her, "I should know better then to push your buttons after what you have been threw." I walked over to her, picked her up and sat her on top of the counter. Before it was time for dinner with our guest, I not only fucked but made love to my girl, just the way that I knew she would love it.

A few hours later, I, Camille, Rose, and her girl Sarah were sitting at the table sharing a delicious meal that consisted of steak, collard greens, potato salad, and of course beans. As I got done with my steak, I decided to interrupt the conversation, "Camille," "yes my love," she looked at me with a smile, "I am going to ask you one time and I want you to be honest with me," "umm ok, what is it?" "How long have you been fucking someone else?" Rose choked on her drink and looked up at me, "I know that you're going to say baby I haven't, and I know that you are lying to me," "I haven't love, I wouldn't do that to you," I twirled my knife in my hands and then threw it into the wall, "I was doing something sweet for you on your phone and I get a text saying "I miss you so much right now baby, when am I going to see you again" and I was taken back because when I looked at the name, all I could think is that you have class and you wouldn't go out of the circle, so either one of you can tell me," Rose just stared at me, "I know that you wouldn't hurt me like this Rose, I'm talking about Sarah," Rose turned and looked at her, "how long?" Rose said.

I got up from the table, pulled my knife out the wall, "three years," "wow, three years of you being an unfaithful bitch," I sat down at the table, cleaned the knife off with my napkin and started eating my steak, "it started with a kiss, and then I just found myself attracted to her, and then it turned into a relationship," "so while I was over there being faithful and making sure that I didn't come back to you in a fuckin box, you were getting fucked by another woman, that's amazing," I chewed my food, "don't you think this is amazing Rose?" "I think it is, I am also wondering how in the hell can you be so calm right now." I placed my knife and fork down, wiped off my mouth and got up, "Baby," "sit down," I yelled at Camille," tears started to come into her eyes, "you see I don't know how I should feel right now," I picked up a vase, "you have my heart, you have every part of me, and you just throw eight

34

years away for some pussy and attention," I suddenly let the vase fly out of my hands and onto the glass table, as it shattered they quickly moved back in there seats, I tried to hold back the tears that would soon be leaving my eyes, "is that better Rose?" "Much," "Do you want some peach cobbler," "I would love some to go," I walked into the kitchen, picked up the cobbler. "Noelle I am so sorry that I hurt you," "you are sorry and I wish that my love for you wasn't so blind." I walked out of the house with Rose and we made our way to our favorite spot and started eating our peach cobbler, "I loved her Noelle, she just moved in with me. What are we going to do?" "I wish I knew Rose, I wish I knew."

Chapter 12

It had been two weeks since I stepped back into the place that I once called my home. I saw that everything was cleaned up, but the hole was still in the wall where I threw the knife. I made my way upstairs and walked into the bedroom, the trash can had tissues in it, the bed wasn't made, there were clothes sitting on the chair. I couldn't help but to clean it up, I quickly made up the bed, hung up her clothes and dumped the trash. Before I left I grabbed my army and EMT uniforms along with some extra clothes. I was hoping to be out of the house before she came back. I heard a little bit of talking and then footsteps making there way up the steps. I started thinking about what to say or what to do. The door opened and in walked Sarah, she stood there as if she was turned to stone. I laughed to myself, grabbed my stuff, and made my way out of the house. "Noelle," Camille said to me as I walked passed her and out the door, "Noelle wait," I stopped and looked at her, "what are you doing here?" "I needed my stuff, I was planning on being gone by the time you got here," "you in a rush to leave," "you don't need me here, you got your new boo waiting in the bedroom," "it's not like that, we aren't doing anything," "you don't have to lie to me," "I'm not baby," "Camille please." I made my way to my car and got inside.

  I really didn't know what to think about the situation because my heart was still in love with her even though it was breaking in a thousand different ways. All I wanted to do was break something; something was eventually going to happen because my temper always managed to get the best of me. *Stay cool Noelle.* I went back to Rose's place and jumped on the computer, I started looking for a place to stay because even though I loved my best friend dearly but I can't stay here because her life is about working, partying, and sex. I am not with that every night, when I work I want to be one hundred percent on the job not half way there. I kept on trying to decide if I wanted to invest my money in a house or just go career in the army. To many things started rolling threw my head, I decided to go for a walk to clear my mind, I stuck my hand in my pocket and pulled out Jena's number *damn I forgot all about this*, I stared at it for a long time *she did say call if I needed someone to talk to*. I placed the number back in my pocket; I knew that it was to soon to be jumping into anything without trying to work things out with Camille first because we share a long life together and I had to try to make it work no matter how much I was hurting because pain is love and real love is pain.

  A couple of days later I decided to go and see Camille, I knew that eventually we were going to have to talk about what happened and see if we could fix it. I parked my car on the street and made my way up the driveway and into the house. I closed the door behind me, walked up the stairs, I heard noise coming from the guest room like something was breaking, I opened the door only to find Camille and Sarah fuckin, "oh shit Noelle," Camille quickly threw Sarah off of her, grabbed a robe and chased after me as I walked out the door. "Noelle," "what?" "I'm sorry," "I came here to talk to you about us, but I don't think you want an us," "Noelle please forgive me, I had a weak moment it wont happen ever again," "it doesn't matter Camille, I am done with there being an us," "just give me another chance to show you Noelle," "once a cheater always a cheater, just forget you ever knew me," "baby please don't do this," "I didn't do anything, you did, you tore us apart, you shattered my heart into pieces," "I feel the same baby," "are you fuckin kiddin me, you don't want this, if you would have talked to me way before this and that bitch wouldn't be in your fuckin bed having every part of that I used to have," "this will always be yours Noelle, I am your wife," "you lost the right to be called my wife when you fucked my best friend's girl," "Noelle…" "goodbye Camille."

Chapter 13
Three months later

I got all clean and fresh in all white with Rose because we had got invited to an all white party, invitation only. There was no way that I could have told this girl no because I had been spending my days getting super wasted until I passed out because it made my nightmares go away sometimes and if I wasn't drinking then I was crying my eyes out or working out. Plus, to Rose doing PT in the morning everyday except for Sunday was not getting enough air. It didn't matter I just wanted to start to forget things and start moving on with my life because it was about time for me to get the ball rolling. For all I knew Camille was fucking Sarah everyday and night of the week. "Tonight you don't think about Camille and I am not going to think about Sarah, we are going to have a good time and enjoy this all white party," said Rose, I started looking her up and down, "you are fuckin sexy," "shut up Noelle," "I'm for real," "please you can't handle this, now lets go." I started laughing and followed her out the door, I loved flirting with her, it would be the highlight of my day sometimes.

Two hours later we arrived in San Diego at a beach house; this was the most beautiful place that I had ever seen. I just don't know if I would have my house decked out in all white like this because if someone spilled something on my shit I would be on fire in a heartbeat. As we walked threw the house we saw so many people that we knew, "it's good to see you in one piece girl," said Tex the gay throwing the party, "it's good to be in one piece," "well you two enjoy yourselves because there are a lot of women that are ready to introduce themselves to you." We hugged one more time and then started to work the room. I couldn't lie, there were a lot of eye candy here that I would have liked to make good company with, but I just wasn't all into it. *What am I going to do? I have to move on this shit is crazy.*

I found myself outside chilling at a table with Rose and some friends around the pool, I hated that they liked to debate about damn near everything, even shit that they knew nothing about. And then they had to start on Iraq, Rose kept looking at me waiting for me to make a comment because some of these people didn't know that I was in the Army. I just sat there and listened to them. "you know what upset me, was this article I read one day, about protestors protesting soldiers funerals," "bullshit," "no lie, they had signs saying "thank GOD for dead soldiers" and "god hates your tears" it is so sad," "its not sad," "shut up Scott you fuckin drunk," "look I am not about to be risking my life for shit, and sacrificing for others is just not going to happen," "that's because you're a bitch," said Rose laughing and sipping on her drink, "fuck you Rose, I know that soldiers you kill be deserve to die and be six feet deep they not helping me," my eyes looked up at him, "fuck them I say, fuck them all, they can all go to hell." I jumped out of my chair and threw the table to the side, and got up in his face, "some of those soldiers happen to be my brothers and sisters that are being laid to rest," "you say that like its my problem," "your problem is that you fail to see that these men and women risk there lives and leave there families to protect people like you," "I didn't tell them to do it, so if they get shot and die then oh well," I pushed him, "you have no idea what its like," "and you do? Do you protect me? Hell no your ass is right here safe and sound in America," "for your information, I was in Iraq not to long ago and I know what its like to lose friends while you are sitting over here on your ass, drinking, and talking shit," "fuck you." I could tell that everyone was staring at us because the conversation had got louder, and I was ready to fuck this guy up, I was trying to remember that he was drunk, but I really didn't give a fuck because my anger was seriously starting to get the best of me at this very moment.

I was getting ready to swing on him when an arm caught me in the air, I stared into the beautiful eyes that belonged to Jena, "Stand down soldier," I couldn't help but to smile and relax a little just by seeing her face, *what is she doing to me?* "I don't think you want to fuck up your life over some drunk dumb ass," "hey fuck you bitch," yelled Scott, I moved passed Jena, made my way over to Scott, "you wanna hit me then hit me, I will have a lawsuit tacked on your ass so fast," I just smiled in his face, "it's people like you that make my life hell and I don't need anymore of the drama and bullshit," I hit him one good time in the face, picked him up over my shoulder and then threw his ass in the pool, "Noelle," Jena started pulling me away, "I couldn't just let him call you a bitch like that," "I could of handle it myself," "there was no way I was going to let you do that," she smiled at me and I smiled back. The next thing I know she took me by the hand and we started walking along the beach under the moonlight, "so why did you have to take care of it for me?" "Because you look sexy as hell in that white dress," "you don't look to bad yourself, your wife is lucky to have you," "is that right?" "Any woman that has someone like you in there life has to be lucky because you're charming, not selfish, and sometimes you put people before your self," "well, I may be the charming and sweet one that some girls want but apparently I wasn't good enough for my wife," Jena looked at me, "I found out that she had been having an affair for three years with my best friend's girlfriend," "then its her lost, she doesn't deserve someone like you," "we been together for eight years," "and three of those eight years were her being unfaithful to you," "I wanted to work it out with her, but my heart shattered," "then its time for you to heal Michaels."

Once we got back to the party I started to feel good about the conversation that I was having with Jena, she is truly an amazing woman, we parted ways and I made my way over to talk to Rose. I gave her the short version of what we talked about, and she was more then excited for me. "Oh shit," Rose tapped me my shoulder as we watched Camille go up and talk to Jena, "what the fuck is she doing here?" "No one knows who gets invited to these things man," "this is not going to be good," "don't tell me you're scared for Jena," "hell no, I'm scared for Camille, Jena is a fuckin black belt dude," "shut the fuck up," "for real man." I started to make my way to where they were, I couldn't believe that this was happening to me, the closer I got the harder my heart started to pound and for some reason I wasn't a fan of this happening to me. "You need to keep your ass away from my wife," said Camille, "last I heard, Noelle is fair game," "bitch you must be out of your got damn mind if you think that you're just going to come between me and whats mine," "she isn't yours, not anymore, you fucked that up along time ago," "you need to mind your own business," "I should say the same," "bitch you don't know me," I jumped in between the girls, "this is not about to happen, not right now," I looked at both of the women back and forth. Jena started heading for the door, "I will talk to you later Michaels," I smiled at her, "that's the bitch from the fucking store," Camille made her way into the house and started calling Jena all types of names, I tried to break it up, I knew that Jena would walk away but Camille just wouldn't let it go. "Damn it Camille stop," I yelled at her and she just looked at me, "we're not together anymore, we are done, you hear me, done," "baby we can work this out," "I don't want to work anything out with you, I fuckin hate you." She stood there looking at me with tears in her eyes, I didn't know what else to tell her, I wasn't going to lie to her about how I was feeling, "just go home Camille, you're fuckin this up for everybody." I turned away and made my way toward Jena, "you will always be mine Noelle always," "Noelle look out," I felt a vase hit me in the back of my head and I fell to the ground.

When I came to everyone was staring at me and then giving me room to get up and breathe, I touched the back of my head and looked at my hand, *she cracked my skull open*, I was helped to my feet and then taken to Rose's car. "I'm sorry you have to leave this way Noelle, I love you girl," Tex said. I sat in the backseat with Jena as Rose drove to the hospital, I knew that I wasn't bleeding to badly otherwise my symptoms would be a lot worst. I think I just needed a few stitches and I was going to be good to go. When we got to the hospital I started talking to some of my friends, which of course got me in a little faster while Rose and Camille waited in the waiting room. "Who did this to you?" "Camille, we broke up sometime ago," "damn girl, you must of really pissed her off," "naw I just told her what she didn't want to hear," "y'all were together for years, no one would easily move on from that," "I know, I just thought that she would have more class when it came to dealing with it," "love makes people do crazy things so you need to watch yourself." I made my way into the waiting room, waved for Camille and Rose, "who is that?" said Rose I watched her turn her head all the way around, "that would be Halle, why?" "Halle is fine, please tell me that she is a lesbian," "why don't you just go find out," "because we're leaving," "I guess you better hurry up then huh," "no, if we're meant to see each other again then it will happen." We walked out of the hospital and made our way back to her place. Jena decided to spend the night and I would take her home in the morning. Rose decided to make her way back to the "hospital" meaning she was going to spend the night at this chic's house to give me and Jena some alone time. I wasn't feeling like anything was going to happen, I offered her my bed but she didn't want it and went to sleep on the couch. I never really met a girl that was willing to do that.

I woke up in a deep sweat, breathing hard, I got out of bed and started looking around my room, "get out of my head," I yelled, I started trashing my room, breaking everything around me. I soon found myself sitting against the wall staring at my door. Jena had walked into my room, closed the door behind her and sat down on the floor with me. "Do you feel like talking?" "No," "then we will sit here until you do because I don't want this to get the best of you." I laid my head on her shoulder, *there really isn't no reason for me not to talk to her, she is trying to help me right now.* "Sometimes we saw dead kids when we would go on patrol, it was hard to stomach, its always hard to stomach, one day we went into this house where we found nothing but dead bodies, when we went down into the basement area there were kids who were shot, we figured they knew we were coming and they not only killed themselves but killed the children as well, and it just broke my heart because it made me think of Brian," "who is Brian?" "My little brother, he risked his life to save another in a shooting at his school and I couldn't save him, just like a couldn't save the unborn child that me and Camille were going to have...my life just seems so unreal sometimes," "this is how real your life is going to get Noelle and I am always going to be here for you if you want to talk," "I'm happy that you're here...when I am around you I feel better, like I am at peace with whats happened." I closed my eyes as she laid her head on mine.

I woke up the next morning, still feeling Jena's head on top of mine, and I slowly moved from under her and stood up. I moved my covers back a little more, picked her up, placed her in the bed, and then covered her up. I quietly made my way out of the room and outside; I started stretching my muscles and then went on my morning run. *Jena seems like a kick ass female, I am just scared that I am going to hurt her and something is going to happen, ugh I really don't know what to do or do I, it wouldn't hurt to just take everything a step at a time, maybe I should just talk to her about it.* When I got back to the house, Rose was getting out of her car, "Whats up girl," "I met this chic last night, she was to die for," "oh yea, what was her name?" "Sanai, we were in the middle of something, the next thing I know she took off," "what about Halle?" "you will just have to introduce me to her when you go back and work at the hospital," "I can do that."

When we walked into the house I saw Jena wearing my favorite pair of sweats and one of my tank tops, Rose hit me with her elbow because she was thinking the same thing that I was. "I hope you don't mind, I took a shower and borrowed some of your clothes," she said, it was hard for me to get some of my words together because for the first time I had actually saw her true natural beauty, "its fine," "you sure?" "Yes," I made my way into my room, I found it to be cleaned and my bed made, *damn this girl been busy.* I started taking a shower, and then got dressed in some shorts and a t-shirt. When I got back into the kitchen Jena had laid a meal out for us to eat, Rose whispered to me, "dude you would truly be a fool if you don't go after a girl like her," we made our way to the table and sat down. "Y'all live like bachelors," said Jena sitting down with us, "technically we are," said Rose, "oh so that just means when you're bringing the ladies home, that's when you make everything nice and orderly," "you know it." I was quiet at the table, I just listened to them talk, *this girl hooked up some food for real she got that southern style to her.* "So, where you from?" I heard Rose enter my ears, "Atlanta," "No wonder your cooking is the shit," "my mom taught me how to cook everything from scratch, she said I should know how to be one hell of cook even if I was becoming a soldier," she glanced over at me, "you're quiet this morning," "I figured I would let my best friend get her interrogation on, so that we wouldn't have to worry about it down the line," "well what if I want to talk to you," "then we will make time for it to happen."

I took her home around 2pm, the ride was quiet, "I make you nervous don't I?" "A little bit," "it's ok to be nervous Noelle," "this is a different kind of nervous," "how so?" "I don't know what to expect from you, everything that you do surprises the hell out of me and I just can't get my thoughts right when it comes to you, you're like a puzzle and the more pieces I get just by being around you, the more I start to want to know so much more about you," "which can't happen because you just got out of an eight year relationship, and you need time to heal, I don't want to pressure you into anything," I pulled up to her house, "Noelle I meant it when I said that any woman would be lucky to have you." I watched as she got out of the car, "oh and Michaels," "yes," "do you still have my number?" "Yes," "maybe you should use it one day, because I'm getting tired of you stalking me." I smiled as I drove away; *she is truly going to get the best of me.*

Chapter 14

  I had finally worked up the nerve to ask Jena out on a date, I was a nervous wreck because I didn't know what I was going to do and to top it off I didn't want Camille showing her face and making a scene. I put on my gray Levi jeans, white chucks, and a white shirt. I stood there looking at myself in the mirror, "you know you're gonna be fine," I looked over at Rose, "dude she likes you and I don't think that there is anyway that you can disappoint her," I took a deep breath, "she is just so simple you know and she is way different then Camille," "don't start that comparing bullshit," "fine." I gave Rose a hug and made my way to Jena's place to pick her up for our date.

  I rang the doorbell, *stay cool, just be calm everything is going to work out fine*. She opened the door and a smile immediately took place on my face, she was wearing black skinny jeans, a nice white top that showed her beautiful round breasts that had a heart shaped necklace sitting in between them. We made our way to my car, and I drove to Victoria Gardens so that we could have dinner at The Hat, this place served you a big meal of food for a nice price. You could get anything like grilled cheese sandwich, ham and cheese sandwich, pastrami burgers, if you could think it most likely they had it. We ordered some chili cheese fries to share with each other, along with two hot dogs. We sat down by window, when our number was called I went to pick up the food while she filled up our drinks. "You didn't think a girl could be this simple on a first date huh," "not really, most of the time its going to Sizzler or Red Lobster or Black Angus, some type of restaurant," "oh so you like seafood," "not really," "then why go?" "Because I would do anything for love," "I think we all would," "so, why is a girl like you single?" "I was waiting for you to ask that, most studs can't deal with the fact that there girl can be just as aggressive as them and some of them couldn't take the fact that I wanted to go into the Army, so this girl I had been seeing for about two years, said its either me or the army, and to me if you love someone you would never make them choose, so I chose the army," "I guess its her lost," "it is because I gave her everything and anything, I can do way better, we both can." After we ate we went to see Iron Man 2 and then movie hoped into Robin Hood, which was something that I was never really able to do with Camille because she would be scared to get kicked out of the movies.

For the first time I held her hand as we walked under the night sky out of the movies, "what do you want to happen between us Noelle?" "I want us to take it slow, because the more time I spend with you, the easier it is for me to move on and let go of Camille," she stopped me and turned me toward her and took both my hands into hers, "when I saw you in Iraq I knew that I wanted to get to know you right away, but I knew that you were taken and that didn't stop me from flirting with you from time to time. And I know everything that you are going threw right now, and I will never hold that against you because the more I am around you I feel like I can fall for you, and I don't want to get hurt in the process if you decide to go back to Camille," "why are you telling me all of this right now?" "Because Camille is right behind you." I turned around and stared her right in the face.

"Noelle I miss you…I wish that things would have turned out better between us with this situation…I am always thinking about you, about how I miss your smile, your laugh, your touch, your kiss, the way we made love…I want you to give us one more chance, so that we can make this work, because my life is incomplete without you," I turned around to look back at Jena but she was gone, *i gave her my jacket to wear and she has my car keys, shit.* I ran over to the parking spot where we parked the car and it was gone, then I felt Camille's arms around me.

I laid down on the bed without a shirt on, feeling Camille kiss my body, feeling her hands move all around my skin, her tongue parted my lips as she shared a long kiss, *something is different*, my hands caressed every part of her body like they used to, I closed my eyes as I felt her start to un-buckle my belt, all I could see were images in my head of her fucking Sarah, of Sarah having her when she was suppose to be my one and only. I stopped her from what she was doing, "whats wrong baby?" she looked up at me, "I can't do this Camille, what was once there for you doesn't even exist any more," "is it because of Jena?" "No, its because I wanted to make things work, I put my heart on the line for you when I came to talk to you that day and all I saw was you fucking Sarah and I cant get that damn image out of my head, my heart shattered that night," "I wish that things could have been different," "me too...I will always love you Camille, you're always right there in my heart but I can't do this with you," "I will always love you too Noelle Michaels," "and I will always love you more Camille Shaw." I kissed her on her forehead, and then I gently kissed her lips, and embraced her. This was the first time that everything had felt so real. I picked up my shirt off the floor and put it back on as I made my way out the door. I as surprised to see Rose sitting out there on top of her car, she tossed me the keys, I jumped in the driver seat and made my way to Jena's house.

"Go get her Noelle, you deserve to be with each other no matter how long the process takes," I kissed Rose on the cheek and made my way to Jena's door. I knocked on it and then rang the doorbell. I could hear music playing slightly loud, my heart was pounding, *get yourself together*. "Hey," Jena said as she opened the door, "you left," "you had to make a choice for yourself," "even though I didn't pay attention to your file in Iraq you still managed to capture me," "Noelle you're not ready for this," "I am willing to take the time if you are because all I know is that I want you," I heard Un-thinkable by Alicia Keys start playing in the ground, I took a step into the doorway, placed my hand on the back of her neck and kissed her lips, she looked at me, and then pulled me in for another kiss, *this feels so right*, we closed the door as we continued to kiss each other, her robe dropped onto the floor, my shirt was thrown on to the couch as we made our way into the bedroom, I laid her down on the bed, she pulled me down to her by my chain "I was hoping you would come," she whispered in my ear, I started kissing and sucking on her neck as I made my way down her body, removing her bra and panties, my tongue moved around her nipple with such grace as I slowly took it into my mouth, my tongue started to trail down her body, kissing each and every part of her, once I reached her pussy I could see her wetness...I slid my tongue between the lips of your pussy and slowly started to taste her as she let out soft moans each time I sucked on her...I started to suck on her a little harder and bit her on her spot...her moans begin to get louder as I slid my fingers inside of her and started fucking her deep, *no strap needed I could handle this*, I continued to suck and lick her pussy up and down, I loved the way that she tasted...she reminded me of a fresh peach...I went harder everytime I heard her say my name and her nails went into my back...I saw her grip the sheets out of the corner of my eye, she arched her back as her sweet juices were released into my mouth and all over my tongue...after tasting her...I made my way up her body kissing her each way, our lips met...we shared a long deep and passionate kiss.

Usher trading places came over the speakers as Jena made her way on top of me and removed my clothing off of my body, "its my turn," she said with a smile. She started grinding her body on my pussy, her hands moved every which way on my body, she even teased me by placing her pussy on my face and letting me get a few licks before she quickly pulled away, she opened my legs a little wider as she started to suck on my pussy, I laid my head back and felt her tongue move up and down my pussy, then I felt her tongue ring *oh shit*, my body started to react in a way that it had never done before, I started biting my bottom lip as she pulled me back into her mouth, sucking on pussy in every way possible, she slid her tongue inside of me and let her tongue vibrate, I felt my body begin to shake as my body started to go crazy and I arched

48

my back *fuck*, she was relentless in stopping every time I felt like I was about to cum...she gently bit on my thighs, as she slid her fingers inside of me and moved her body up mine. My moans were uncontrollable...I swear she was in tune to the song because as soon as it hit the part with Usher singing the moans I was right in tune with him...I grabbed the back of her head pushing her face into my pussy so that she could taste my juices, as I screamed her name. I just felt myself go higher then ecstasy...as my body started to calm down from shaking and feeling her inside me she kissed up my body and laid her head on my chest...I wrapped my arms around her and held her tight as I laid there on cloud nine.

The next morning I woke up feeling good, Jena kissed me on my chest "where do we go from here?" "I don't want no other girl but you, I just want to see where this path takes us...no pressure," "no pressure," she kissed me on my lips, then made her way out of the bed, I watched her walk around in her nakedness, as she turned on some bath water. She got back in bed with me, laid on top of me, "I know that this isn't the most appropriate time to ask but what happened with you and Spade out there?" I moved her off of me and sat up in the bed, "*we took cover behind the vehicle, we had Hinson radioing for help where we were, but it seemed like we were surrounded by so many of them, it was an ambush and we were trapped. We fired our weapons like crazy, but it didn't help that we were in the sand and the sky wasn't that clear for us to see, so we started throwing grenades, in opposite directions, as we started to move around the vehicle Spade grabbed me and took four bullets in the chest...once the smoke started to clear the Calvary had arrived, I didn't let Spade go, we talked the whole ride back to our camp, and the last thing he said was to tell his mom that he loved her and that he died a true hero, and all I could think was that I am not going to let him die not in my arms like my brother did...by the time we got to the base we were to late...the day of his funeral I told his mom the story and how he saved my life, she said "that sounds exactly like my son, never selfish and putting others before himself" she even said that she knew about me because he told her about all of us,*" I looked up at Jena,

49

"everything else was just dead bodies blown to pieces my mines or bombs that went off, it was some nasty shit..," she placed her finger on my lip, took me by the hand and led me into the bathroom with her, where we got into the bath together. I laid my back against her chest, "how do you feel right now?" "I feel better, I feel like the more I talk about it sometimes, it makes me warm up to it a little better and helps me cause less destruction," "the thoughts will always live in your mind, just control it better and you feel better with each passing day." I felt her lips on my neck; I laid my head back and relaxed in her arms.

Later that night I went back to Rose's house, where she was entertaining some company as always. "How did it go?" "Less just say for the second time in our friendship you were right," "GOD always has a plan for people like you Noelle." I walked into my room and sat down at my desk; I opened up RealPlayer on my laptop and started looking for something to listen to, I put on a play list that I had made, it held a mixture of rap, R&B, and rock songs, I turned the music up and started rocking out to The Fray Absolute, as the smile on my face stayed there permanently, I couldn't wait to see Jena again, she was becoming so much more then a friend to me.

Chapter 15
Three and a half years later

I had just got back into my newly bought house from walking the dog. We made our way upstairs and into the bedroom, I pulled off my hoodie and threw it on the chair. I crawled onto the bed and cuddled up next to Jena.

About two and a half years ago when we were all sitting around talking, I had finally got the courage to ask her to be my girlfriend. After about a year and a half we bought a house together because we were damn near living with each other anyway. And to top things off we always talked about starting a family. So right now Jena is carrying my seed inside of her along with our child; she is seven months pregnant. I know it seems like we didn't waste anytime starting our family, but this was something that we wanted and we knew that our future was with each other and not anyone else because we both would have walked away a long time ago.

A few hours later we made our way to Ontario Mills Mall, I was really hoping that we didn't go into every store in this damn place…we made our way into the converse store to look at shoes, "I thought you were going to stop wearing these," Jena said looking at the selections of shoes that they had, "I just want to see what they have baby," "you always say that, then you buy a pair," I looked back at her and smiled. I ended up buying a Yoshi type green pair of shoes. "You know I got these for you," "no you didn't," "I did," "shut up Noelle," I wrapped my arms around her and kissed her on her neck. We walked into Bebe, The Levi Store, Forever 21, and Victoria Secrets before we finally came back to where we started.

We sat down at the food court trying to decide what to eat, I was sure that Jena wanted damn near everything in here. Luckily she kept it simple and chose Sabarro, I went and got three slices of pepperoni pizza, a salad, and some bread. I made my way back to the table and we started eating. "You're Rose's only family, huh?" "Yea you could say that because once her parents found out she was a lesbian they kicked her out the house and really didn't care after that, her story is a little deeper then this," "oh ok...what about your parents?" "They were never really around to begin with, I always have there support in whatever I do though," "that's good, my mom and dad are still together living in Atlanta," "do you want to move back to ATL?" "I have thought about it from time to time but my life is here with you," "if you ever want to relocate then just say the words and we can make it happen," "would you really leave Cali for me?" "I love Cali always and forever but I will always love you more."

Before we left the mall we stopped in the Candy Factory, I got a bag of Boston Baked Beans and she got some gummi bears...we walked out of the mall and back to the car, I sat the bags on the ground, opened Jena's door, gave her the key to start the car and put the air on as I put the bags in the trunk of the car. I jumped into the driver side of the car, "you look tired baby," "I am, my back and my feet are killin me," "when we get home we will take a warm bath and then I will give you a massage," "aren't you just as sweet as you want to be." I smiled as I put on my seatbelt.

As soon as I backed out the car, another one smashed straight into us on Jena's side, *what the fuck*, I got myself out of the car, and spotted Camille jumping into another car and speeding off. I went back into the car to check on Jena, "talk to me baby, talk to me," I checked her eyes as she looked around, I checked her pulse and anything else that I could while she was sitting here, "just hang on baby," I didn't want to alarm her by telling her she was bleeding between the legs, but I was sure that she felt it, I didn't even hear the ambulance pull up, Chris pulled me out of the car and he helped the fire department get her out of the car. I jumped into the back with her as we made our way to the ER at Kaiser. Once we pulled up to the hospital her heart stopped beating, the nurse held me at the door as they rushed her inside, I waited in the waiting room wondering where the fuck Rose was.

"Noelle," I looked up to see Rose walking into the room, she didn't say another word to me just embraced me as I started crying once again in her arms. She had helped me calm down and told me that everything was going to be ok, just be patient and wait. "I have to tell you something," Rose said, "please don't tell me you're getting married," we both started laughing, "naw girl…you're getting deployed again the letter came today," she handed me the opened envelope and I just sat there in silence.

Chapter 16

I walked into the room and was met by Jena's smiling face, the good news was that our baby boy was going to be just fine and the bad news was that I had to go back to Iraq. "I know that look Noelle," she said softly, "You have to go back, don't you?" I shook my head yes, "I know you don't want to go but you have no choice but to go, your unit needs you, you are the one that they trust," "I want to see the birth of our child," "you and I both know whats going to happen if you don't go." I sat on the bed next to her as her hand rested on my thigh. "I've been thinking about what we should name our son," "whats that?" I took her by the hand and looked at her, "Brian Spade Michaels," before I could ask her why she answered it for me, "you love Brian more then anything so its only right that he is named after his uncle...I say Spade because if it wasn't for him you wouldn't be here right now and I believe that our child should carry your last name." she moved her fingers threw my hair, "and maybe one day Brian will have another sibling," "give me a daughter that looks just like you and my world will be complete." We shared a gentle kiss as I let her lay back down and get some rest.

I sat outside resting my head on my hand, letting everything that has happened in the pass 24 hours sink into my mind. All I could do was wonder why Camille would do such a thing, part of me just wanted to hunt her down and kill her. But I knew that it wouldn't end in my favor.

Two days later I was able to take Jena home, I got her some of her favorite food that she was carving, and then I let her order me around when it came to packing up my gear to leave for Iraq tomorrow...for the rest of the night I laid there in her arms with my hand resting on our son. *I can't believe this is really happening right now.*

The last words that continued to echo in my mind was I love you, there was no come back home to me or don't fuckin die out there it was just those three simple little words that made me feel like I was standing on top of the world. We both understood that nothing was ever promised when going to Iraq; I just hoped that I made it back to my family safe and sound.

As Rose dropped me off at the station that I would be leaving out of, I started to feel a little paranoid, "I want you to move into my house in the guest room," "what for?" "I don't know what Camille is capable of at this point and I don't want to lose my family," "I got you," "I'm for real Rose, take care of our family, that's your god son in that oven," she smiled at me, "nothing is going to harm my family, I would die before I let anything happen to them," "lets just hope that it doesn't come to that," Rose looked at me like I was losing my mind. I pulled my bags out the trunk, gave Rose a hug and made my way inside.

Chapter 17
Two months later

Cooper hooked me up with a web cam while we were in Iraq so that I could watch the birth of my child; I owed her so much for this. I watched Jena push for about four hours before Brian came out crying his lungs out and when I saw her hold him for the first time, all I could think was that I had to make sure I got back to my family, my beautiful family. He was so innocent, peaceful and beautiful. I couldn't wait to see his eyes open, I was hoping they were green like his mothers or they could be light brown like mine, it didn't really matter though.

I sat on my bed looking at the ring that I had bought for Jena, I was thinking that when I got back and everything seemed calm and normal that I would give it to her. My heart was already on the line since I landed over here. I put the ring back on my dog tags and let it sit on my heart as I went to check my email because we were getting ready to head out soon for a night patrol.

Noelle,

I know you think that when you come back home you might walk into some big secret like you did with Camille, I just want you to know that I am nothing like her. Because I feel that if you truly love someone and you are head over hills in love with them, then sleeping or even talking to another woman should be the last thing that you are doing. And it shouldn't even be a thought in your mind, because how can you be in love with someone and you're fuckin someone else? But anyways, I will never leave you unless you give me a reason to, and it hasn't happened yet. I miss you and Brian misses you, I can't wait for you to hold him in your arms. I can't wait to see you when you get home as well…my love is forever yours.

Jena Mayfield

P.S. when you get a chance listen to Trey Songz- Yo Side of The Bed…I love you SGT Michaels.

I kept looking at the time as I pulled the song up on Youtube, I plugged in the headphones, and started listening to the song as I started to write her back at the same time…I finished the letter as the song came to an end, and as I made my way to go on patrol with my boys the song played over and over again in my mind along with the words that I had wrote her…

Jena,

If someone told me that after getting seriously fucked over in my eight year relationship that I would find someone like you, I wouldn't believe them because not many woman will wait around for you to get your shit together. And I know that you took a chance on me because you saw something special inside of me that I really wasn't seeing in myself at the time. And as I listen to this song it makes me miss you that much more because every night when I close my eyes I see your face and feel the warmth of your body next to mine. There is no way that I will not come to you and Brian, my heart is filled with so much love for the both of you…I love you and miss the best of you so much, and just like the song said, I'm comin back baby, I am always coming back to you because you give me every reason to live.

SGT Noelle Michaels

For You I will

Just the Beginning…

At first glance you might think damn she sexy, I wonder if I can get her number?
I'm most likely thinking the same thing as we smile and walk pass each other.
In most cases, if you take the time to get to know me you will see that there is more to me then what meets the eye.
You will find that at a young age I live my life to the fullest, because you'll never know when it will be taken away.
You will also find that I love the outdoors, I love being in nature.
To me it is the true essence of being in beauty itself.
In any case I believe that everyday we live, breathe, walk around on this earth, and do what we love.
That we are creating our own story, our own history, something that we can look back on and think *damn, I did that*.
But nothing could prepare me for the series of unfortunate events that were about to occur in my life.
My name is Adrian Coolidge and this is my story.

Every morning at 5am me and my bestfriend Natasha would wake up to go running, we would run up hill so that we could see the sunrise and then make our way back down very carefully. Most people would talk during a time like this, but we just complemented each other with our presences. I had known Natasha all my life; she is the most beautiful girl that I could ever lay my eyes on. I never had enough courage to tell her that I love her, that I was in love with her. I valued our friendship to much and I didn't want it to be destroyed because I couldn't control my feelings. There were times where I thought she felt the same way because she would always talk about me and other females or me always having a lot of females around me. I couldn't help that they liked what they saw. I wouldn't give in to them though, I seen them with some of my friends and heard all kinds of shit about some of these girls that I wasn't trying to catch anything. And even through the mist of it all, the only girl I continued to see in my dreams and when I was awake was Natasha.

I sat across the kitchen table glancing at her from time to time, as we ate breakfast before we went to school. My mom was always up cooking and trying to stay busy. For some reason her body couldn't click with the idea that she was 6 months pregnant with my baby brother. I had to hand it to her though, she kept things nice and neat around here, while I was gone to school and my dad was at work. We looked up as my dad walked in and kissed my mom on the cheek, grabbed some toast and went out the door. I never understood why almost everyday he left in a hurry like he was going to be late or that some morning meeting was taken place that he just had to get to. But I really didn't focus too much on him; I was more worried about my mom being home alone for long periods of time. At times I wouldn't even go out because I wanted to make sure that she was ok, and that nothing would happen to the baby.

A few hours later I was sitting in a chair along with my peers on the football field, it was graduation day. I was excited knowing that my mom was sitting in the stands cheering for me, but I didn't want her to cheer to hard and the baby pops out. I swear it took forever to just walk across the stage and get a piece of paper for twelve years of hard work. And then you have to turn around and embark on another four years to get your Bachelors. Once all the seniors had got there diploma and the principal told us congratulations, we all threw our caps in the air and begin to hug each other. Some of my friends were heading straight into the service, and some were going to school out of state. I was only going to miss a hand full of them, everyone else just didn't matter to me that much. The parents were soon let on to the field I ran over to them and embraced them; my mom was crying more then me.

Later that night, I laid on my bed thinking about what I was going to do next. Everyone thought that I might move or go into the Army myself. But I don't think that I wanted to do that at the age of sixteen. I still had two years to not have my parent's signature on things. "Adrian, there is someone at the door for you," my mom yelled. I got up and made my way down the steps and to the front door. "Oh shit, whats up Billie," I hugged her so tight, "what are you doing here?" "You know I wasn't going to miss your graduation." Billie was about two years older then me; she always had my best interest at heart. When she graduated she moved to New York to go to school. Damn I missed that girl. "So how have you been? What are you going to do?" "I'm ok, I was just thinking about that," "you know you can't wait to make a move, there are to many opportunities out there. You have to go and get them," "I'm not like you Billie, I just can't pack up and leave," "I know, but you still have a future to look toward. It's better to know now, then to discover it when you're forty. You just have a driven spirit, no one or nothing can stop you."

Billie had crashed on my bed, I didn't even bother to go to sleep because it was time for me to meet up with Natasha for our run. I quickly changed my clothes and walked down to her house. "Good morning," I said to her as she made her way down the driveway, "good morning." We started walking down the street. Natasha grabbed my hand, "whats wrong?" I looked at her but nothing came out of her mouth. We just walked up the hill and sat in our spot. "I'm moving on Saturday, its for my dad's job, I just found out today," "we were suppose to celebrate with each other," "I know, I'm sorry," "it's not your fault." She laid her head on my shoulder; I wiped her tears away as I laid my head on top of hers.

The next morning, I got up super early to get a jump start on cleaning the house. I wasn't about to have my mom doing this while I was gone. First I washed the dog, then the car, and watered the grass. I washed down the tables in the house, the windows, mirrors, and anything else that you could think of. Then I went into the kitchen and cooked my mom some breakfast. "knock, knock," I said as I opened her bedroom door, "aren't you a sweetheart," "I try." I sat the tray down on the bed and laid there with her. "Where's dad?" "He had to go into work," "oh," there was no way I was going to tell my mom that I didn't see him leave, "so you're going out tonight?" "Yes ma'am," "I want you to be careful and don't get into any trouble," "you know I'm always careful mom," "I used to say the same thing at your age, and then some years later I crashed my motorcycle into another car because the guy I was racing didn't want to get beat by a female," I looked up at her, "you're my daughter, I know what you are up to," "I can't keep nothing from you can I?" "Some things you can, and others you can't."

I had got dressed and ready to go out and party, I went into my parent's room, "what do you think?" "You look good," "thanks mom, what time you want me home?" "Lets say no later then two-thirty," "ok mom, I love you," "I love you too, you be safe out there."

Before I knew it, I was listening to my Ducati shake the streets as I raced against this guy for two-hundred dollars. I loved the adrenaline rush that I got from speeding down the street, turning the corners, and feeling the air on my skin. When I crossed the finish line, I popped a wheelie and then brought my bike to a halt. I quickly took off my helmet and collected my money from the loser. All night people were racing on the street, the police wasn't going to get involved because the house wasn't in a community type area. My homie Gina, had bought a race track for cars, and on the other side she built a street racing track for motorcycles. She also had a two-story house built so that she can live by what she loves.

I walked into the house, the music was blasting like we were in a nightclub, and everyone was dancing, and having a good time. I stood there drinking some punch, and rockin my head to the music. "Is that all you're going to do tonight is stand here?" "I thought you had a flight to catch," "my dad saw how upset I was and let me have my last night out before we left," her hands wrapped around me, and I could feel her heartbeat on my back, "come and dance with me." We walked out on to the dance floor; her body was so close to mine. We danced to every song that was being played, I gently kissed her on her neck, while my hands rested on her hips, our bodies were in tune with each other. Natasha turned around and faced me, our eyes locked on to each other, we leaned in closer, our lips begin to touch, "Adrian," I heard one of my friends yell, "your mom is outside looking for you." I walked with Natasha outside, "you be safe out there, I'm going to miss you," "stop frontin, you got all your females here to keep you company," "you know you're the only one for me, without you my life would be in ruins," "whatever Adrian," "I'm for real, without you my world is chaos and I lose myself, you are what keeps me grounded," "you tell that to all the girls," "only the ones that I love."

I smiled as I got into the car with my mom, "do you know what time it is?" I looked at the clock, "I am so sorry, I lost track of time," "I figured you did, considering Natasha was here," "what is that supposed to mean?" "That you have more then just a crush on her," "awh mom," "what? Look at you turning red like an apple," "How come dad didn't come and get me?" "He wasn't answering, I called his office about five times and his cell about ten," "you shouldn't be out here like this," "I just wanted to make sure you were ok, because you weren't answering your phone either," "I had my hands full," "yea, with Natasha." We both started laughing as my mom stopped at the light. "I love you mom," "I love you more Adrain." As the light turned green my mom took off, and instantly we were hit by another car. It pushed us half way down the street and we crashed into a wall. My vision was blurry and I kept blacking in and out. I looked over at my mom, I couldn't tell if she was moving or not. Eventually my eyes just shut, as I held her hand.

Beep. Beep. Beep. Beep. My eyes started to move to the sound of my heartbeat, I slowly opened them. My vision was a slight blur. I looked around my room. *what the fuck happened?* Soon my dad walked in with the doctor, I was told to sit up and cough as they removed the tube out of my mouth. I drunk some water and then sat there. My dad just stood there looking at me, as tears came down his face, he walked over to me, kissed me on my forehead and then walked out of the room.

Two days later I was able to go home. It felt good being able to go outside and not just walk around the hospital. The ride home was silent; my dad still hadn't said anything to me and drove me crazy not knowing why. But I wasn't going to force conversation on him. We pulled up into the driveway, my dad jumped out of the car and went into the house, *so much for getting help*, I slowly got out of the car ad started making my way up the driveway. Every step was more painful then the other, I thought that I was going to fall over and die. When I had made it to the steps, I sat down to catch my breath, "welcome home," said my Aunt Christina sitting down next to me, "it doesn't seem like much of a welcome, my dad hasn't said two words to me," "so that means you don't know what happened," "all I remember is I went out Saturday night, my mom came and got me because I had lost track of time, and then we were in a car accident," "do you know what today is?" "Sunday, June 12th," "how about, November 16th," "No way," "you were in a coma for five months," "What about my mom?" my other auntie had came out the house and handed me the baby, "this is your brother Isaac," "what happened to my mom?" "She passed away and two weeks later you woke up." My auntie hugged us and left, I handed Isaac to my aunt Christina and started making my way to my room.

I sat on the floor facing the window, I didn't want to see or talk to anyone, "Adrian its me Billie," she walked in and closed the door behind her, "you know your mom was by your side everyday and night, reading books to you and singing to you, praying that one day your eyes would open. She was so stubborn, she made the doctors give her a bed in your room," she sat down next to me, I fell into her arms and cried my eyes out, "why couldn't it have been me?" "Because GOD still has plans for you," Billie helped me get into bed, "Can you stay with me?" "I knew that you were going to say that, I brought my bag just in case." I laid in her arms, thinking about what had just been said to me.

I went out into the backyard and gave Natasha a call because Billie said she was trying to get a hold of me, I knew that hearing her voice would make me feel ten times better. "Hello," "it feels good to hear your voice," "Adrian!! Oh my God, how are you?" "I'm hanging in there," "that's good to hear, but I will talk to you later," "why? We just started talking," "my girl is here and I don't want to be rude." We got off the phone and I couldn't believe what she had said.

Two months later…me and my dad didn't really speak to each other a lot, it was a hi or how are you or I'm leaving. I stood over Isaacs crib looking at him, I picked him up, I told him that I was going to tell him about our mother and how kick ass she was. Because he deserved to know apart of her, even though he didn't know her that long, "put him down," said my dad, "why can't I hold my baby brother?" "Put him down, now!!" he yelled at me. I placed Isaac back in his crib. "What is your problem?" "You are my got damn problem, I want you out of my house tonight," "what did I do to you?" "You took my wife away from me, you took my heart and soul and buried it six feet deep." I stood there looking at him, and then made my way to my room; he walked in behind me and started pulling my clothes out of the drawers and closet. I sat there, as he knocked pictures off of my wall, ripped pictures of me and my mother together, "you don't deserve to see her face," he yelled at me. He stormed out of my room; I could hear him talking to someone and then my auntie Nina walked into my room, "you are going to stay with me until your dad heals a little better." I helped her with my belongings and left the house.

Leaving with my Aunt Nina was like living in a prison in hell. Not only was she strict, but there wasn't a day that went by that she didn't have herself a drink and say "you should be dead not my sister," "I fuckin hate you, you killed my sister," "it's your fault that she is dead." It was being said so much that I was beginning to believe it myself. This lead me to my first drug, I started smoking weed just to catch a high that would take me from all the drama and bullshit. Everytime she cussed me out, I took a hit, and soon it became a ritual to me. Almost immediately, things started to get worst, she would come into my room at night, yelling at me and calling me all kinds of bitches, she would kick the bed and throw her vodka bottle against the wall. I started not sleeping at night because of that. This lead me to my second drug, cocaine, I loved the way that it entered my veins and filled my body. It got so bad that I started to put that shit on my cereal.

I started spending more time with my boy Kirk, he was a known drug dealer on the block, he let me stay with him anytime that I wanted. "Yo nigga, I don't know why you just don't pack your shit up and move in here with me, you here every fuckin day," "the thought had crossed my mind," "shit girl, you always welcome here, you pay for your drugs and shit, you don't fuckin steal from me, and you keep shit clean," "you sure man, I don't want to impose on your space," "shut the fuck up nigga, go get your shit and bring your ass back here." He threw me the keys to his to BMW, I got into the car and went to my aunties house. I went inside and started packing all of my clothes before she had got home from work, I even took a picture of my mom. Right when I was about to walk out the house she came in, "where in the hell do you think you're going?" "What does it matter to you? You don't want me here anyway." I placed the key to the house on the table, walked out the door, put my bag in the backseat, and left.

Living at Kirk's house was like an everyday party, all I did was smoke weed and do lines of coke with him. This lead me to my third drug, ecstasy, that shit made me feel so good and for some reason it turned me on to the fuckin max. I started sleeping with girls that I didn't even fuckin know, I felt like I was becoming a guy, just getting my pussy licked by any bitch who offered. Kirk granted me immunity with his boys, he said I didn't have to get jumped into the gang and that I could slang for him as long as I wanted and nothing would come back on me. I took the deal because I needed the cash. After I popped my pill I saw my phone ringing, "What up Natasha?" "You tell me, what are you doing hanging out with Kirk?" "He helping me in my time of need," "what is that noise in the background," "Kirk is having a party, and I need to get back to it, my females are waiting for me," "it's like that now," "yea, I thought you knew," "what the fuck happened to you?" "You have no idea, and you never will." I hung up the phone.

I always go and see my grandmother when ever she calls, plus it was the only way that I could see Isaac, I missed him so much. As soon as I walked into the house, I hugged my grandma, "What are you cooking grandma?" "Oh not much baby, just some collard greens, corn bread, ham, sweet potato pie," "why so much?" "My grand daughter need some meat on her bones, and I know that you haven't been eating right, staying with that Kirk fella." I walked into the back room, and held Isaac, he had gotten so big since the last time that I had seen him. He was going to be a year old in a few months. "Adrian, come on in here and eat," I kissed him on the forehead and placed him back in his crib. I sat down at the table, "what are you going to do with your life? yo're going to be eighteen this year," "I don't know what to do," "you listen to me, you used to me driven and so passionate about things. It wasn't just you doing photography or drawing, it was you doing what you loved and what made you happy." After I was done eating, I washed the dishes, saw my bro one more time, took the plate that my grandma had made for me, "Adrian," "yes grandma," "go and visit your mother." I walked out the house without saying a word, haven't been to her grave sense I found out she was dead. I popped two X pills and made my home.

"Where you been dwag? Bitches were coming over here lookin for you," said Kirk, "I went to go and see my grandmother," "how she doin?" "Good as always," "look, we gone do a run tonight," "you always took Max with you," "that dude is so fucked up on meth, that I don't even want him around me," "I feel you." I walked into the house, went to my room, laid across my bed and went to sleep. I woke up to Kirk calling me, letting me know that it was time to go, I put on my shoes and jacket, walked outside and rolled out with him. We pulled into the parking lot of a nightclub and went inside; we went all the way to the back room. "Trey, this my nigga Adrian," I shook hands with the guy. We sat down and I listened to them discuss business, as two of his men went outside and loaded up the car. Two hours later we were walking out the door.

I sat on the couch back at the house, "yo Adrian, you gone need this," Kirk handed me a gun, "what for? I'm not doin this to stay in," "yea right, you bring in more money then any of these fools that have been workin for me for years," "we have a deal man," "and I am goin to keep my word, but I want you to be protected, cuz once fuckers around here start hearin about the new hot shot, they gone be gunnin for you," I took the gun out of his hand.

It wasn't before long that I found myself behind a restaurant, beaten the shit out of some guy with the back of my gun because he tried to rob me. Kirk said this was how I earned my stripes, by showing people that I wasn't a punk and that I didn't take shit from nobody. We went back inside from the back; I went into the bathroom and washed my hands. Then I followed the waiter to the table that we were sitting at. "That's how you handle shit Adrian, you go hard or go home," "I feel you, no one is goin to bow down to me," "if you stay in this shit, you gone be my right hand, you comin up in the ranks like a true soldier." We sat there eating our dinner, then I saw I familiar figure, her long legs, athletic shaped body, a smile that made the sun jealous, her brown mocha skin, and eyes that held her true story. *What was Natasha doing here?* I turned my head as she walked passed me, and continued with my business. After we were done eating, I waited outside for Kirk because he was taking care of the bill, "look who it is, Adrian Coolidge," she made her way over to me, "whats up?" "Not that much, how have you been?" "Excellent, and yourself?" "Great, I'm waitin for my girl to come out," "that's nice," "yea it is, we just got engaged," "well congrats, I wish you the best," "thanks, you know can come to the wedding," "no thank you," "why are we like this Adrian?" "You have your life and I have mine, we grew apart and moved on with our lives," "it wasn't supposed to be like this," "how was it supposed to be?" "We were supposed to be friends forever, and always be there for each other no matter what," "well, that was gone a long time ago." I lit my cig, "it was good seeing you," I got into the car with Kirk and he took off.

I took a girl into my room, I took off my pants and my boxers, sat on the bed, slid my pussy to the edge, and the girl went to work on me. I laid my head back as I smoked my weed, enjoying everything that was happening to me. Then I heard arguing coming from the other room, *fuck I hope this shit doesn't ruin my mood*, then I heard some glass break, I pushed the girl off of me, put on some shorts and walked out my room. I was a few seconds to late because Kirk had shot Max two times in the chest, he wiped his nose and looked at me, "bastard was stealin from me, for all these years," he shot him again, "I wouldn't think in a million years he would do this shit to me," he wiped his nose again and put another bullet in him, "damn it Kirk he dead," "help me get him in the car," "I can't do that, I'm not helping you." He walked over to me, wrapped his hand around my throat, and put the gun to my face, "you are going to do as I say, not as you fuckin please," "I can't man, his blood can't be on my hands," blood dripped from his nose, "yea your right, you to young for this shit," he stepped back, took out a blade and cut down his arm, "this my word in blood, you help me, I say nothing and if I do, you can tell his bro that I killed him and he will kill me." I stood there looking at him, thinking, not only did he kill the competitions brother, he is losing his fucking mind. I had nightmares for a month, after helping him get rid of the body.

That lead me to my fourth drug, PCP, it just felt good taking it from time to time when I didn't want the shit that I had been taken. And everyday I found myself driving pass the cemetery. I felt like shit every time I didn't go and see her, I felt like I was passing her by and acting like she didn't exist. Drugs, money, and women were starting to become the center of my life. I started to keep myself in the dark, stayed wearing sunglasses so that no one could see my eyes, I only went out when I had to, otherwise I was nothing more then a ghost in the night.

I laid back in the chair, with some girl kissing on me, even though she was there, it felt like she wasn't. I was getting tired of seeing some of the girl's everyday, wanting me to fuck them or for them to fuck me. My pussy wasn't even wet half the time. "Get off of me," "why baby? I thought we were going to fuck," "didn't you just fuck, my homeboy last night," she looked at me and then got up. I still didn't play that, I don't know what these girls or guys up in here have. I even made it part of my ritual to sober up for a bit and then go and get tested and get my shots for all of these STDs that were floating around, because I was not about to be a victim.

While chillin at a house party, I got a phone call from Natasha, "hello," "how are you?" "Same a before, whats up?" "Nothing, I just wanted to talk to you and see how you were," "you could of sent me a text for that," "Adrian, I'm tryin to save you from yourself," "you can't save someone that doesn't want to be saved Natasha," "why don't you want to be saved?" "because this is my life that I am living and I love it, it is the best thing that I could have ever accomplished in my life," "being a drug dealer is not an accomplishment, its asking for death to come to your door and take you away," "maybe that's my destiny, to be a drug dealer, live my life to the fullest, make money, fuck girls, and then die," "what happened to the girl that I used to be in love with?" "She died the first day I called and you didn't talk to her because you were to busy, and then my heart broke even more when I found out you were engaged," "are you blaming me for your life being shitty?" "No, I'm thanking you for killing me, you see ever since that day, I have been yelled at, kicked out, blamed, destroyed, anything and everything that you can name. Kirk showed me a whole new way to live, he opened my eyes to so many things. That is why you will never understand the pain that I feel. So save your tears, go be with your girl, and leave me the fuck alone." I didn't let her say anything to me; I just hung up the phone.

After I got off the phone, I spotted Kirk getting into an argument with some people. I and two other guys walked over to them. We stood watching as they started fighting because

71

once one of them jumped in we were jumping in as well. Kirk threw the guy on the ground and started stomping on him like he was nothing more then a bug, soon one of his boys jumped in and tackled him to the floor, I pulled the guy off Kirk and started beating him with my gun. Before I knew it, everyone around us was fighting, then a gun went off in the sky and we all started running, bullets were being shot threw the crowd as we all ran to our cars to get the hell out of there. Kirk unlocked the doors to the BMW and we all jumped inside, he started speeding down the street for a good 5 mins before he finally slowed down. "Adrian you're fuckin bleedin man," I look down at my shirt, "I didn't even feel it hit me," the guy in the back seat took off his shirt and placed pressure on my side. "Oh shit man, the police is behind us," Kirk pulled over, "just try and keep yourself together when he comes to the window." I held my composure as best as I could while the officer took his information. When he walked back to the back, "just hang in there man," "Kirk she about to go into shock," "what the fuck do you want me to do?" "I don't know, but she can fuckin die right here." The cop came back to the car, gave him his information back and told him to get his tail light fixed. *How the fuck do you have a light out on a BMW?* Kirk parked on the grass of the house, they took me out the car, placed me on my bed and one of his doctor friends started to take care of me.

When I woke up, my vision was blurry and I was seeing double of everything. The doctor had given me some Vicodin to take for the pain. Guess what my new drug became? That's right, Vicodin, they don't tell you that this shit is highly addictive. All they say is take this twice a day or before you go to sleep. Not hey be careful you can get hooked on this. There were times where I would just sit in the house, doing nothing because I was so fucked up that I couldn't even walk. I had lost every reason to stop eating; I just no longer carried a taste for food. I just wanted my weed, X, PCP, cocaine, and Vicodin. Those became the new loves of my life.

I am standing in a subway, which is slightly odd because California doesn't have those. I am standing in the middle of two angles, one is decked out in all black and her wings are even black, the other angel is in all white just like

72

her wings. They are both calling to me. The angel in white is saying "it pays to be good," while the other says, "being bad feels so good," "you have to pull yourself through this," "you are fine right where you are," "your life doesn't have to be this way," "you make your own rules and do as you please," "go and see your mother," "continue to do what you are doing," "don't lose yourself in this chaos Adrian, this is not what your future holds," "Adrian, don't listen to her. You go and have all the girls you want, make all the money you want, and gain all the power and respect that you desire," then a bright light flashed on my right and fire on my left.

I woke up feeling hot, sweaty and shaky. I didn't understand what was going on with my body. That was the second time that I had had that dream. It was like GOD and the devil trying to get me to go there way. I knew that I had a decision that I had to make. It was either going to be life or death for me at some point. But the life of a drug dealer was greater then anything that I have ever known, I was making mad money, having and getting any chic that I wanted, I had respect and power, and I put fear into people because of the job that I do. It made me more powerful then I could imagine, and I loved the feeling. I loved the rush even more. I reached over and grabbed my bottle that contained my X, I poured two pills into my hand. I looked at them for a long time and I started to hear the voices again, "don't do it" it whispered to me. I just popped the pills in my mouth, drunk some punch and then laid back down in my bed. I started to feel better, but my vision started to get a little blurry. I just closed my eyes and went back to sleep.

A ball of fire enters my mind, as I see a female figure walk out dragging a chair. She conveniently sits in the chair backwards and just sits there staring at me while I am sleeping. I feel my body start to get hot. My breathing starts to get heavier, I feel like I am being suffocated. Her eyes soon turn red, "never forget me." Her face turned into a demon as she jumped at me.

I jumped out of the bed so fast, ran to the bathroom, and jumped into a cold shower. I let the cold water run all over my body. I put on some shorts and a white beater, and then walked out the bathroom. "What the hell man?" "I felt like my body was on fire," "you want to try some of this shit?" "What is it?" "Heroin," he stared at me, as he held up the needle. "I don't do needles," "this shit is poppin, I'm telling you," "I don't want it, I got all the shit I need in there," "if you ever change your mind, it will be right here." I walked back into my room and sat on my bed; I grabbed my sunglasses off of the nightstand, put them on, and then grabbed my cocaine and weed. I went outside and sat on the porch. I lit my weed, took a few puffs and then I did a line of coke.

I found myself walking down the street, just to take in some fresh air, "Adrian, yo Adrian," I turned around to see Billie running over to me. "Where have you been man?" she gave me a hug, "just here in there, how have you been?" "Oh man, I've been great. I just got a few of my businesses up and running. I'm just tryin to stay busy," "that's good man, I know you always wanted that," "how have you been?" "I been great," "have you really?" "Yea...why wouldn't I be?" "I just hear that you've been runnin with Kirk and dealing drugs now," "it's just extra cash in my pocket," "you could always come and work for me, and you can move in with me," "I got a place to stay and I have a job." Kirk's car pulled up to where I was standing, "Adrian...," "it was good seeing you Billie," "same here." I got into the car. I looked over at Kirk as he was driving, it seemed like something was heavy on his mind. Then he turned off road and started speeding down a dirt trail. Shortly after a few minutes, he came to a screeching stop. He got out the car, came over to my side and pulled me out. He slammed me against the car, "I trust you my nigga," "I know you do," "I know that you would never do me wrong, right?" "Never...what the fuck is wrong with you?" "Nothing, I just want to make sure that we're on the same page." I stood there staring at him as he started to pace back and forth.

Back at the house, I laid in my bed looking up at the ceiling, I was trying to piece some of the things that have been going on in my life. I closed my eyes for a brief second...*this is not you Adrian, living your life with such destruction, what would your father think? Oh wait he doesn't give a shit about you. Laughter filled my dreams.* I opened my eyes and popped some Vicodin and washed it down with some Jose. I lift my shades up and rub my eye, I hear someone walk into my room and sit down on the bed with me, "Are you ok Adrian?" they started to rub my shoulder, "I'm fine," I felt their arms wrap around me, "you don't look like you're ok," "I am excellent, now please leave my bedroom," "can I just stay until you fall asleep?" "No!! I want you to leave now." I felt their lips touch my skin, I tried to push them away from me and get up, but the drugs were taking hold of my body. "I'm gonna take care of you Adrian." The last thing I remember was falling backwards into my pillows. I started to slowly come to, "fuck her pussy is tight," I couldn't make out the voice, "shit feels so good," I felt something push deep into me, "she is so fucking wet," my eyes slowly started to open, "oh shit." I felt a fist go across my face and knock me out.

I woke up holding the side of my head, *damn how fucked up did I get*, I slowly slid off the bed, *shit that hurts*, I place my hand between my legs as I slowly got on my feet. I make my way out of the room and into the bathroom. As I begin to undress I sit down on the toilet and throw my clothes on the floor. I noticed blood on the shorts that I was wearing. *I know this isn't my period I just had it*, I put my clothes back on and go to my room. I pull my sheets back, and there lays a fresh stain of blood. I stood in my doorway looking at everyone in the house, *what the fuck happened? Who was I last with? Was I really just fuckin raped?* "Are you ok Adrian?" said Swift as he walked up to me, "I don't know," "what do you mean?" I could always trust Swift when it came to talking about personal issues; he was like my big brother. I took him into my room and showed him the blood, "it's ok sis, I'm going to find out who did this shit…and when I know something so will you," "thanks Swift," "anything for you, I don't believe in hurting women, and I will put a lock on your door so that niggas can't get in," "Swift, you don't have to do all of that," "I know I don't but I want to…you go get yourself a smoke, I will clean this up for you then I'm going to take you to the hospital," "I don't have any insurance," "I got you covered, my girl is a doctor there."

I sat on the porch twirling my weed in my hand, "are you going to smoke it or play wit it?" said Kirk walking out the front door, "umm I'm going to smoke it eventually," "you seem all lost and shit," "I'm good." Swift walked out the house and I followed him down the steps. "Where you niggas goin?" yelled Kirk, "can't a nigga eat." We both got into the car.

Swift sat in the room with me as we waited for the doctor, his girlfriend, to come into the room. It felt weird being in a gown, sitting right here half naked, all I wanted to do was get dressed and tell Swift lets roll. I kicked my feet back in forth, the wait seemed like forever. "Hi Adrian, I'm Doctor Shay," "hi," "I'm going to have you lay down, and you are going to place your feet up for me, so that I can check your vaginal area and then I am going to do some blood work to make sure that you didn't catch anything," "is it going to hurt?" "I'm not going to lie to you, it can be painful...Swift come and hold her hand." Swift got up, stood next to me and held my hand, "its going to be ok sis, I'm right here, squeeze as hard as you want." My eyes begin to water as I felt her take swabs from my pussy, then she stuck this duck looking thing inside of me, I just wanted to kick her in the face, I squeezed his hand so hard. When she was done, I sat back up and looked at her. "You were raped and you do have some scaring down there, do you know who did this to you?" "Naw babe, she doesn't remember. But I am going to find out, there are a lot of fucked up niggas in our inner circle who would of loved to get a piece of her," "just bring me a sample of there spit, anything, so that we can make an accurate match," "you know I will." I watched as they kissed each other and make there way out of the room. I started to slowly get dressed; *I can't believe that I was raped.*

Every night before I went to sleep, Swift would come and check on me, he wouldn't leave until I was knocked out, and he always locked the door every time he left. I was surprised to meet a guy like him that did shit like this, it was rare. "Swift, why do you do this?" "I had to be a man and take care of my family, paychecks weren't coming quick enough, this was quick and easy money, it helped me keep my house and a roof over my girl and kids head, I'm not gonna be here forever.

I held my phone in my hand, just staring at Natasha's picture, part of me wanted to call her and the other part made me feel like she didn't want to talk to me ever again. I just had to know. I listened to the phone ring in my ear, *maybe she won't answer*, "who the fuck is this?" "Adrian, who are you?" "I'm Natasha's fiancée," "Can I speak to her?" "She busy right now," "will you let her know that I called?" "Why do you need to talk to my girl?" I just hung up the phone.

Kirk walked into my room and placed a pill bottle in front of me while I was rolling up my weed; I looked at it, then at him and continued to roll. "My homie said this shit is stronger then cocaine, and since you do that shit, I figured you might want to try something a little stronger." I watched as he got up and left, lit my joint and started getting high. Two hours later I popped two X pills. Two hours after that I did a line of coke. Before I went to bed, I took two shots of tequila and some Vicodin. I laid in my bed high as a kite.

I watched as a black panther walked in front of a group of people, there were five of them; my head turned as they walked pass me. One of them looked back and winked at me. Soon they started running and took off into the sky, when I turned my head back I was face to face with the panther.

"Hey grandma," I pulled myself out of bed, "Did you forget that today is your brothers birthday?" "No, I'm on my way over there right now," "ok." I quickly got dressed, I ran out the door, jumped into the car, and drove to the mall. When I got there I went straight for the shoe store. "Adrian," I turned to see Natasha staring at me, "hey," "what are you doing here?" "its my little brother's birthday today," "you forgot?" "you know how I am with dates," "yea I know," "I called you sometime ago, your girl answered," "I'm sorry if she talked shit to you, she trips like that sometimes…ever since we got engaged its been like a hole different world," "as long as your happy that's all that matters," "true." For the first time in a long time I started to feel that feeling that I thought was lost, we picked up two pairs of shoes and an outfit for him to wear. We even managed to sit down and have lunch together. "I got something for you," she placed a box on the table, "what is it?" "Your birthday present…I carry it around with me hoping that I would run into you one day to give it to you," "my birthday was four months ago," "I know...I waited." I opened the box up, I pulled the locket out and opened it, "I know that it seems cheesy, but I just wanted you to always remember that I..." her phone started to ring and she quickly answered it, "hey my love," "I'm at the mall," "I will be home soon," "no I'm not spending a lot of money," "why are you acting like that," "fine, I'm comin home now." I watched as she got up and left without saying anything to me. I quickly picked up my bags and chased after her, "Natasha," I grabbed her by the arm and turned her around to face me, tears were running down her face, and all I could do was hold her in my arms.

Finally, I made it to my grandma's house. I walked up the driveway and knocked on the door. My grandma let me in, "someone looks happy for once...you must of saw Natasha," "grandma...please." I walked into the room where Isaac was, I couldn't believe that two years had already passed, he was walking and talking a little bit. I picked him up as he gave me a big hug. Then I helped him try on his new shoes. I just sat there looking at him laugh in play, it made me think about my mom and how we would always play together. "What the fuck are doing here?" I looked up only to see my dad standing there, "didn't I tell you to stay away from him," "I didn't know he was here," "get the fuck out of this house," "this isn't your house, you can't kick me out of here," "you really think I give a fuck," he grabbed me by my arm and dragged me out the house, my grandma yelled for him to stop, "its ok grandma, its ok." I hit the concrete and then jumped to my feet, "you stay away from my son," "what did I ever do to you?" "You took my wife from me, you took everything and I will not let you influence my son," "where the fuck were you that night, huh? Why didn't you answer her phone calls when she called you? You should have been there, not her...what the fuck were you doin? Were you fuckin your secretary while your wife and daughter were fighting for there lives, huh? How long was it before you got to the hospital?" he walked up to me and pushed me, "I was there as soon as I got the fuckin call at my office," "so you could answer then, but not when mom was calling you to come and pick me up?" he hit me so hard across the face, but I stood my ground, "don't you ever question me about the things that I do," "why? Because you're not the saint that you make people think you are?" "Because I'm your father, and you will respect me," "how can I respect someone who doesn't even respect me, how can I respect my father when he cant even respect his daughter, how can I continue to love you as my father, when you no longer have love in your heart for your own daughter…maybe it would benefit you more, if I just died right now." I looked over at my grandma, looked at my father, "I love you dad, no matter how much you hate me." I took a few steps backwards, then turned around and walked to my car. I sat there for a few minutes, started the car and then drove back home.

I sat in the driveway, I felt so shaky at the moment, I started looking for all my drugs inside the car, and then I ran inside the house and into my room. I popped open the bottle that I kept my cocaine in and poured it out on the desk, I smoothed it out as quick as I could and then did a line of it. I sat there rubbing my nose, still feeling shaky, I stared at the bottle that Kirk had gave me not that long ago. I picked it up, started turning the bottle around in my hands, the voices came back to my head as I poured a tablet into my hand, *don't do this Adrian, you're going to burn if you do*, "get the fuck out of my head," I yelled and then tossed the tablet into my mouth. As I looked around I started to see shit, *how did these birds get into my room*, I opened the window and tried to help them get out, then I ran out of my room and into the living room, "get the fuck down, everybody get the fuck down," "what the hell?" "You didn't hear the gun shots?" I started looking out the window with my gun out, "look out the window, don't you seem them," "there's nothing out there," said Kirk, "what the fuck is wrong with you?" "They're out there, they know what we've been doin, we gotta fuckin get them," "no one is out there, why don't you sit down." I started smiling and looking around the room, birds were flying, "look at the birds, they are so beautiful," I got up and walked out of the front door, "Adrian…you need to come back inside girl, that shit I gave you wasn't what I thought it was," I pointed my finger, "look at the angles," "damn it Adrian," Kirk stood in front of me, "it's an hallucinogen…this shit is way stronger," "what you give me man?" "LSD…I need you to come inside," "I wanna go with the angles," "there are no fuckin angles." Kirk tried to pull me back into the house, I pushed him off of me and ran toward the angels, as I started to run so did they, I looked back and Kirk was chasing after me. I jumped over a gate, and continued to follow them. I ran up the stairs to a building, I watched as they stood there with there wings out, "I'm going to go with the angles Kirk, I'm going to be fine," "there is nothing there, so I need you to come off of that ledge right now," "look at there wings, so big and black, she is holding her hand out for me, she wants me to go with them," "Adrian," "don't step any closer Kirk, you can't stop me from doing this," "listen to me, in twelve hours it will all be over," "you don't understand, I see them all the time in my dreams and they talk to me like they are doing now." I placed my hand in the hand of the angles, "take me with you, I wanna go with you," "who are you talking to?" "I turned and look at Kirk, "for the last time…I am talking to the angles." I felt myself flying with them, "Adrian," I heard Kirk yell. My body felt so free as I went into the air and we dropped down into fire. The last thing I heard was something crashing.

I opened my eyes and stood up, I was standing in a desert, I looked all the way around, and see nothing or no one. "Hey," I looked to my left, "come over here," "who are you?" I stood in the same spot, "let's just say I'm the evil side of things," "you mean like the devil?" "Yea, he is my master," "why am I here?" "This is where you belong, on the dark side with us," "because of all the things that I have done," "you would be correct," "so this is hell?" "Not really," "then where am I?" "You are what we call a rare commodity, you see you have a choice to make between us and them," I watched as she pointed to an angel an all white. "I don't understand, am I dead?" "Not yet," said the angel in white, "you are slowly dying." I looked at both of them as they stood in front of me. "Maybe I can help you understand," "why don't you stay out of this?" "Because GOD hasn't given up on her yet," "this is mine, why don't you and your GOD go somewhere else." They faced each other, "I am not here to fight you," "I don't give a damn." Fire surrounded them as I took a few steps back, I watched as they begin to fight. There wings came out of there backs and they took to the sky, I watched as the dark angel got slammed into the ground, she got back to her feet and moved so quickly toward the white angel that she flew backwards. The dark angel threw a ball of fire at her, and it hit her skin, she touched the ground and it begin to turn into water, and plants started to grow from the ground trapping the dark angel. "Enough," I heard two voices say at the same time, the veins broke from around the dark angel, and then they both disappeared.

I walked over to the hole that was in the ground, it looked like a bomb had went off, I picked up the feather that laid there on the ground. When I turned back around both angles were standing in there spots. "I am Ky, I am the leader of the fallen soldiers, we are the most elite team for the devil. And we want you to continue to walk this earth, and continue to be the voice for the devil. We will in rich your life with whatever you desire, as long as when you die your soul walks through the gates of hell." "I am Niyah, I am the leader of the guardians, and we are the prestigious team for GOD. We want to offer you a second chance at life, all you have to do is do better, get your life back to where it should be. We will not in rich your life with material things because you will have gained so much more then that. And when your time has come, you will be judged and then welcomed into the gates of heaven." They disappeared once again, but this time two pathways appeared before me, one was for the good and the other for the bad. I made my choice.

I felt myself take a breath, my head felt like it was spinning and my vision was blurry once again. I watched the nurse come in, and then she ran out the room. I saw the doctor and Billie come into the room. After the doctor took a quick look at me, he left the room. "You should be dead right now," she looked over at me with tears in her eyes, "if it wasn't for some young man walking out of his office and finding you, you would not be here," "I was with Kirk," "Kirk wasn't there, it was just you," "they said that you jumped off of a building like you were flying, and then you hit the car with so much force, that the impact alone should of killed you," she wiped her eyes and got a little closer to me, "and if that wouldn't of killed you it would have been the drugs." Tears left my eyes, I didn't like to see her cry like this, "I don't know what to say," "say that you are going to go and live with her and get better," I looked at my doorway and saw Swift walking in, Billie had briefly left the room. "Has anyone come to see me?" "No one is going to step foot in here, they only care when you're out there with them, helping them make money," "they said we were a family," "they lied to you...the only people that you are around right now are those who truly love you, those who are your true family." I just laid there letting silent tears leave my eyes; I just wanted to jump out of the bed and go talk to half the fuckers who claimed to always be there for me no matter what.

Billie lived in a two-story house with her girlfriend, Roslyn; she was a model and was currently in Brazil doing a spread. So I wouldn't meet her for a cool minute. Most of the time when you walk into people's houses you either see white, tan, or gray walls. When I walked inside her house, I was hit with a ray of colors throughout the house. Pictures of Billie's work complemented the walls as she gave me the tour around the house. We made our way upstairs and stopped in front of a door, she pulled out a key and handed it to me, "check it out, I will be in there in a minute to check on you. She went into her room, and got on the phone, I could tell she was talking to her girl by the way she sounded. I unlocked the door and walked inside, the walls were depicted as a forest with a waterfall over the head of my bed, and there were motorcycles in various places in the painting. "I figured I could complement your love for nature and motorcycles into one," "you didn't have to do this," "I know, but I wanted to. It's rare that I could do things for you, your like my sister, I love you," "I love you too man," "I will let you get some rest, and I will see you in the morning." I sat down on the bed continuing to look at my new room, thinking *I can't believe this is mine*, I kicked off my shoes and laid down on the bed. *I hope that I made the right choice on getting a second chance at life.* I took a deep breath, closed my eyes, and went to sleep.

The next day I woke up to birds chirping outside my window, I moved down to the foot of the bed, and looked up at the sky. The sky was clear and beautiful; I could tell that it was going to be a warm day, a perfect time to go to the beach. "Damn man I thought you would never wake up," Billie said as she walked into my room, "so what do you think? Beautiful weather, a nice sunny day, maybe go and chill at the beach?" "Sounds good to me," "then hurry up and get ready so we can hit the road." I got out the bed, made it up, took a shower, and then got dressed. I jumped into the passenger side of the Jeep, and started to put lotion on my legs. "I was hoping you shaved," "shut up, I'm not a guy," "you could of fooled me," "I don't know if I could mess with a girl that didn't shave her legs or armpits, it just seems weird," "but in some cultures they don't," "I know, but still." After a little while we arrived at the beach…we walked across the hot sand until we found the perfect spot to sit. I watched as people played in the water, kids build sandcastles and bury each other in the sand. "When was the last time you came to the beach?" "when I was with Natasha…we would come early and run, as soon as the sun started to come up we would cool off in the water, then go and get some ice cream," "I can tell that you miss her," "besides my mom, she was the only woman who I felt cared for me, and you can see that my dad treats me like shit now," "hopefully you guys could work it out, because life is to short," "I agree," "I'm going to go get some sun block," "ok." I looked at my hand and it was trembling, I left so fast that I didn't even get a chance to take a hit. *I hope Billie doesn't see me shaking like this, fuck.* When she came back we went and took a dip in the water, then I buried her in the sand and took pictures.

When we got back to the house, I helped unpack some of the things that we had taken with us, then I ran upstairs to my room, locked the door as I closed it, pulled my stash out from underneath my bed and took a line of coke and popped an X pill. I did a quick inventory of what I had, *damn this might only last me about two weeks if I portion it out right.* I placed the box back underneath my bed, I sat in the chair with my sunglasses on, letting my head hang down as I felt my high take over my body. Billie would kill me if she knew I was doing this shit in her house, I couldn't let her find out because I know that I am wrong for doing it here. And to top it off I have to give her more respect because she gave me shelter and a job as her assistant so that I could get myself on my feet and not be out there in the cold. I at least owed her that much for her gratitude.

4 weeks later, all my shit is gone, I started to work out to try and keep my mind off of it but it wasn't helping. The worst part of it all was that I had just started working for Billie and I just couldn't sit still for nothing, I sat at my desk tapping my fingers on the book that was sitting there and just zoned out. "Adrian...Adrian," "whats up?" "Are you ok?" "Yes," "you sure? Because you been zoned out all day and kind of shaky," "I'm fine...I'm just nervous, I don't want to mess up what you have built," "dude, don't be crazy...you're not gonna mess up anything you have to much self control...but you do need to relax," "I will try." I started walking around and talking to the customers about the paintings that they were looking at, I brought the paintings to life, because sometimes it was better to hear it then to read it. I saw Billie watching me from her office as I worked the room, the smile on her face was priceless, "I knew you could do it," she mouthed to me.

Later that night, I left the house and went to the homies house where they were having a house party. I greeted a few people as I walked inside; I searched through the crowd looking for my friend and a girl that I could get off with. "Yo man where you been," said my friend coming up to me, "around...I need you to hook me up with my regular shit," "I got you man, just pay before you leave, I will have it ready for you," "load me with some weed," "enjoy man, this is that real shit right here," "nothing but the best for you." I gave him some love, and started looking for the girl I had just saw. "I saw you looking at me," I turned to see her standing next to me, "I was checkin you out as well," "whats your name?" "Candice," "pleasure to meet you," "likewise," we started dancing to Usher's Hey daddy. When the song was over, we went into a back room and started blazin. Candice started stripping to the music that was playing, after she undressed herself she undressed me, I let her hit a few puffs before she started to lick my pussy. I laid back and enjoyed myself. When she was done, I returned the favor, I let her hold the blunt while I ate her pussy…2 hours later…we started walking out of the bedroom, "call me baby," she handed me a piece of paper and walked away. I stuck it in my pocket, went to go get my merchandise from my friend and then made my way back home.

2 months later…I sat at the table eating a bowl of cereal that had a little bit of cocaine sprinkled on it. "Hello," I heard someone say as they walked into the front door, I heard steps run from upstairs, down the steps and then some kissing noises. "Adrian come here," I got up and walked into the living room, "this is my girl Roslyn, Roslyn this is Adrian," "nice to finally meet you, I have hard so much about you," "likewise." We chatted for a few minutes then they disappeared upstairs. I decided to leave because I wasn't one to listen to people have sex. I went to go and visit my grandmother and stayed over there for a few nights. It was hard being there because I didn't know when my dad was going to pop up and I didn't want her to endure another argument.

"There goes your baby," said Billie pointing to Natasha walking out of the store, "with her fiancée right be side her," "she getting married?" "I thought you knew," "nope, every time I talk to her its mainly about you," I turned and looked at her, "I'm for real, she said she had a girl but not a fiancée and from what she was telling me, something is wrong with her girl," "I got that vibe once as well," "I think you should go say hi," "I can't," "why not? she is practically your wife anyway," "because if her girl says something to me I don't know if I will be able to hold my tongue, let alone keep from stomping her the fuck out," "true, you do have a temper like that," "true love never dies Adrian," said Roslyn, "and I believe that her fiancée would be more jealous of you, because she will see the connection that you two share," "I don't want to create conflict between them," "as if you care," said Billie laughing, "you never cared about the girls she was with, you would just hurt, like you are now, but its more extreme," "true, very true."

We started walking around the mall, we were in Rancho because Roslyn liked going to Victoria Gardens, it was the

85

only outside mall that I knew existed out here. We walked into JC Penny, I tried on a few leather jackets. "It looks good on you," said Natasha, "thanks," "so why is it that I always have to be the first one to make a move," "what do you mean?" "I know that you seen me, but you don't bother to talk to me," "you have a girl now, so I don't see a point in speaking to you," "why? I thought we were friends," "we are I just don't have much to say to you…it would be a lie to act if I am interested in you getting married to someone else," "what are you saying Adrian?" I took off the jacket and put it back on the hanger, "nothing," I started to walk away but I was stopped by Billie and Roslyn, "tell her how you feel." I looked back at her standing there, "I told you that without you my life would be in ruins, and ever since that day I found out you had a girl and you just got off the phone with me for her my life has been hell…it hurt my heart to know that you were laid up with someone else, that I served no importance to your life, it even hurt more thinking about how everyone else got to be with you, and I was left on the sidelines. Then when I found out you were engaged, I was like damn, I was so far gone, that my life truly had become hell and I lost myself …I don't like you talking about some other chic, I don't like seeing you with an engagement ring on your finger…because I'm not the chic that you're talking about and I am not the chic that you are going to marry," "why are you just telling me this now?" "It wouldn't have mattered when I told you, because no matter how many times we flirted back and forth, held each other at night, and shared precious moments. You would always end up being someone else's girlfriend…it was great seeing you Natasha and happy birthday." I walked out of the store and back into the sun, I put two X pills into my mouth as I walked to the truck, I pulled down the back and sat down.

Billie and Roslyn joined me on the back of the truck, they just sat there in silence, "at least she knows how you feel now and you've been wanting to do that forever," I just sat there with my arms crossed and tears coming out of my eyes…5 minutes later…I lifted up my glasses and wiped my eyes, "I guess that no matter what happens, if it is truly meant to be then she will come back to me," "the question is, how long are you willing to wait," "I will give her a year, because I still have some shit in my life that I have to get together before I can even let someone in." we sat there for a bit longer, and then started to hear people arguing, we look all around the parking lot trying to see who it was. Then we saw Natasha and her fiancée arguing. "Damn I can't believe they are arguing in public like this," said Roslyn, "me either, I never heard her yell like that," I said. Our mouths dropped when we saw her hit Natasha across the face, I jumped off the truck and ran in there direction as I saw her hit her again. I tackled her to the ground and started punching her lights out, "Adrian stop, stop," I heard her yell, then I felt Billie pull me off of her, "what the fuck is wrong with you?" "No one puts hands on you like that, that's not love," I yelled at her, "I know that she loves me…it was just an accident," I watched as she helped her up and wiped the blood from her face, "I can't believe you," "I will catch you in the street partner," "I'm right here man, do something." Her girl tried to come toward me but Billie kept her at bay, "take Adrian to the car," "Natasha…she doesn't deserve you, she doesn't love you," "shut the fuck up man, me and my wife belong together," yelled her fiancée. I sat in the backseat of the car, I didn't know if I was should be sad, angry or both. I placed two more pills in my mouth, placed my hand over my heart. What had been shattered has been stepped on and turned into pieces. "Do you feel better?" said Billie, "I feel like shit," "I meant hitting the fiancée," "oh, that felt great," "I bet it did, you are one crazy mofo," "I warned you," "I know," "what are we going to do now?" "Get something to eat…I'm starving," "aww our little fighter worked up an appetite," we all started laughing.

Although I felt like my heart had shattered into pieces, I still felt the same love for her; I couldn't deny what was real between us. I knew that she felt the same way; I just didn't understand why she would turn on me like that so quick. We are the true definition of love. I just don't want her to wait until it's too late to figure it out.

I stopped doing some of the drugs that I was doing because it was becoming to much, I just stuck with weed, X, and cocaine. Those were my drugs of choice, so when I didn't have one, I always had the other. It was hard going from making thousands of dollars in a week to a few hundred, but I made it work for me because Billie was investing a lot in me and I didn't want to be a disappointment...I woke up to my phone ringing, thinking *who could be callin me at this time*, I saw that it was Natasha. I sat up in my bed, and answered the phone, "hey," "whats up," "I was sleeping," "I didn't mean to wake up, I just wanted to talk to you about the other day," "what about it?" "I should of never done that, I know that you were just looking out for me," "don't worry about it Natasha," "I have to Adrian...I love you," "what?" "I love you...you are such a big part of my heart and I dated other people just to see how true it was. And everytime I came back to you, but I didn't believe that it would happen time and time again," "and then you met your fiancée," "and then you got your females," "and I neva lost you," "and I neva lost you either," "what do you want to do?" "I just want to let our path come to a full circle," she paused for a minute, "I have to go now." She hung up the phone and I sat there staring into nothing.

    3 months later...I found myself with my back against the bed, a girl between my legs, and a joint in my mouth. I started to lose myself in the pleasure that I was feeling, until my phone started to vibrate. I looked at it and saw that it was Natasha, again. I didn't understand why she was calling me that much and at the same time I didn't know if it was her or her fiancée. I just sat my phone back down and laid my head back, I wasn't about to let this get ruined. Ugh. I started not to enjoy myself because Natasha was putting in an effort to talk to me and I was brushing her off for some pussy. And the sad part was that it wasn't even that good.

    Back home, I felt like shit, I popped a pill and sat in the backyard looking up at the stars. "you're up late" said Roslyn sitting down next to me, "I couldn't sleep," "I couldn't either...so you know Billie speaks highly of you," "I don't know why," "she believes in you, and she knows that you can do so much more then what you are doing now," "I will get on the right track in time," "Adrian, you can't sit around and wait for things to happen on there own because when you do you learn the hard the way," "as long as I learn something," "but a hard way is not always a good way, when you can start making the change now," "every night I close my eyes and dream about angles, every night I get pulled seven different ways, because I don't know which way I want to go, all I know is that in the long run I want to be happy," "and you believe that drugs and havin one night stands every night are going to make you happy?" "It did when I started," "and what about now?" "It just seems like a regular thing to me, like showering and getting dressed in the morning," "I have faith in you Adrian, and I know that whatever path you wish to take we will be right there by your side. Because you never give up on a friend, you just give them a push every now and then." Roslyn got up and kissed me on my cheek, then made her way back into the house. I know that you can't save anyone who doesn't want to be saved or help anyone who doesn't want to be helped, but they never said anything about getting a push every now and then from a friend. Here I am with a chance to make a difference in my life and I really don't feel up to it, everyone is always telling me to go and visit my mom but I am to scared to. It's been so long. I'm sure if my mom is one of those angles that I see in my dreams every night then I know that she is not pleased at what I have become. I took a deep breath and felt myself drift off to sleep.

I woke up to the birds chirping in my ear, and I was wrapped up in a blanket. I starred up at the morning sky, this was the first time in a long time I had went to sleep under the moon and woke up with the sun. I stretched and moved the blanket off of me; I got up and made my way into the house. "I gave you the blanket because it cold last night," said Billie handing me a plate of food, I went and sat down at the table. "Your phone has being ringing off the hook, I just put it on silent and plugged it up in your room," "thanks Billie," "and your grandma called me, and I think that you should call her back because she sounded upset." After I finished eating, I went and jumped in the shower, and called my grandma back. "I need you to come to the hospital," she said in a frantic voice, "why what happened?" "Your dad is in the hospital," "I don't give a damn," "he is asking for you…he has been in here for three days already, and I knew you wouldn't come. But he is dying," "then let his ass die he doesn't want me anyway," "did you not just hear me say that he wants to talk to you, he wants to see you, and you need to come down here anyway because you have to get your brother." My grandma hung up the phone on me; I made my way downstairs and told Billie what happened. We all made our way to the hospital.

Once we got there I found the room that they were in, I hugged the life out of Isaac and then I was left alone with my father. I sat in the chair that was beside his bed staring at him. I watched as the nurse walked in, "what happened to him?" "He was injured by a beam at work, they said the wires had come a loose while he was walking threw the site." As she left I sat there in silence, thinking about how it was when I woke up, he wasn't even this close to me, and he was so distant. I watched as he opened his eyes slowly, I stared him right in his face. "Why were you asking for me?" "I have to tell you something," "what?" "I was acting out toward you because I was more mad at myself about what happened and a placed the blame on you," "why didn't you answer when my mom called," "I was busy…having sex with my Sophia," "your secretary?" "Yes," "so your're telling me that while me and my mom was getting into an accident and fighting for our lives you were fuckin your secretary…what kind of shit is that?" "Adrian, I had a weak moment," "you were strong enough to fuck her," "don't talk to me in that tone of voice," "I can talk to you how ever I want…you fucked up and I paid for it," "I never meant for it to get this far, I am so sorry," "sorry isn't going to give me my life back and it damn sure ain't gonna bring mom back," "Adrian…" he yelled out, "I don't have time for this," I turned around and walked out of the room. Everything that he said echoed in my mind over and over again. I quickly walked into the bathroom, popped a pill, and gathered my thoughts before I went back in front of my family.

On the ride home, I held Isaac in my arms as I talked on the phone to Natasha, letting her know what had just happened. I felt like things were slowly starting to come together. I had a good friend in Billie and Roslyn, they were helping me out so much and I didn't even have anything to offer them in return. No matter what I thought or said they always said "you can stay here until you die." I would spend a lot of time outside with Isaac; he had a lot of energy, now I see why my grandma wanted me to take care of him. "I feel like this is finally home," said Billie sitting down and handing me a drink, "I have my sister here, my little brother, my future wife, and when we are ready we are going to give Isaac someone to play with," we looked at each other and smiled. "I owe you big time for this Billie, I don't know how I'm going to repay you," "just do right by your brother and get your life together," "I think that I can manage that." After a few hours of running around, he came and laid down on me and went to sleep, "you can't keep him out here all night," said Roslyn "I'm not, I am going to take us to bed soon." I waited a few more minutes, then picked up Isaac, carried him inside the house, and we both went to sleep.

I woke up with the little guy next to me, I was so afraid that I might knock him off the bed or something. He was laying there staring at me, "lets get you showered and fed," I picked him up and took him into the bathroom, ran him a warm bath to play in for a little bit after I washed him, I put his clothes on him, let him stay with his toys as I went downstairs to the kitchen to get him some food. As I made him a bowl of cereal I saw Billie and Roslyn doing laps in the pool, I swear they are fishes. I made my way back up to my room...I slowly sat the bowl down on the desk...I slowly walked toward Isaac...my heart was racing as I saw him holding my X pills in his hand and a bag of coke in the other hand. "Isaac, look at me," he turned his head and smiled, I watched as one of the pills almost entered his mouth and I grabbed his hand so fast. He started crying and I held him close to me, trying to get him to calm down.

That night I sat in the backyard crying to my hearts content, Billie sat next to me the whole time not saying a word. "I need help man...I want to get help and get better." She held me in her arms, and at that moment all I could think about was Natasha and how she would hold me when I was down, that just made my tears flow even more.

Two days later...I found myself in rehab, I was in a room all alone, sweating out this shit, losing my mind because all I wanted what a hit of my all time favorite pill or maybe cocaine. I never thought that withdrawal could be like this, I felt as if I was losing a major part of myself. I was angry, I was sad, I just wanted to leave. But I knew that I had to stay not only for me but for my brother.

One month later…I knocked on the door of the doctor's office, "come in," I heard her say, I walked inside only to be greeted by a 5'7, short haired beauty with a booty, "I'm Dr. Charal," she said shaking my hand, "I'm Adrian." We both sat down in the chairs as I admired her cherry wood furniture, and not to mention her body, *damn the things I would do to her.* "So, Adrian let's talk about how you are feeling today and where this all began," "I can't do that," "why not?" "because I don't know, I want to know about you just like your going to learn about me," "but this isn't about me Adrian, its about you," "no disrespect, but I know that there are people out there in the world that tell a stranger things that they never even told there bestfriend, I'm not one of those people." I watched as she placed her notebook down along with her glasses and crossed her legs. "My name is Amy Charal, I am from Miami, I moved to Cali about 10 years ago and I have been here ever since…anything else?" "I noticed that you have a tattoo…how many do you have?" "You're cute," she said laughing, "I had to ask…when I see a woman with tattoos, I think it's the sexist thing ever," "I have 18," "nice," "now can we get back to our session," "my name is Adrian Coolidge, I have been doing drugs since the day I went to live with my aunty, my father recently passed away and I didn't give a damn because he was cheating on my mother and he blamed me for it…anything else doctor?" "You have a lot of hostility," "I am a very angry person right now," "I can see," "I don't want to talk about this right now," "what do you want to talk about?" "You," "why me?" "Because you are my doctor, and I think that if you are helping me threw this process I should know more about you," "I feel like you're hitting on me," "that's because I am," "I have a girlfriend," "what does she have to do with me?" She looked at me and smiled and all I could do was smile back. As we sat there, I noticed a picture on her wall, I got up and looked it, I saw Billie's name on it, "my friend painted this,"

"Really? You know Billie Rockwell," "not only do I know her, she is like my big sister," "I love her work, I have two of her paintings in my office and a collection of some of her work at home," "that's whats up, would you like to meet her?" "I can't have a relationship with my patients outside of work," "we're not, we are just two people who love art, and may end up being in the same place at the same time, two weeks from today Friday night at 8, the Gallery on Hollywood blvd," "I think I know where that is," "you should its practically the gay city of LA," "can you sit down please so that we can finish our session." I sat back down in the chair and we started talking more about my life, but in the back of my mind all I could think about was laying her across her desk and having my way with her. I knew from this point that I was going to enjoy every session that I had with her.

I was looking forward to the next session that I was having with Dr. Charal because it had been 3 days since we had last spoke. I made my way to her office and knocked on the door, "come in," I heard her sweet voice say, I couldn't help but to stare at her ass while she was looked in her file cabinet, "damn," I said under my breath, "did you say something?" she turned around and looked at me, "nope." I sat down in the chair and watched her. Part of me just wanted to stand behind her. Eventually she came and sat down, and we started to talk about my life problems. It seemed like everything that had happened to me up until this point I was telling her, it made me really sad when she told me that I should go and see my mom. When the session was over she walked me to the door, "I have been meaning to tell you something," "what do you need to tell me? You know that's what I am here for," "do you promise not to get mad?" "I promise, I am here for you, whats going on?" I took a deep breath, leaned in and kissed her on her lips, she stood there looking at me, "see you next session," she said to me as she made her way back to her desk and I walked out the door.

Friday night…I never had to deal with so much work before; Billie had me running around town, making sure that everything was in order and coming in on time. There was part of me that just wanted to say fuck it and duck in an alley to have a smoke, but I quit that shit. And I had to remember what I talked about with the doctor during my sessions. I made my way back to the gallery, "Adrian, you need to go and talk to Billie she is going crazy in there," said Tyra, "whats going on?" "I don't know, she just came out of her office and started talking shit to everybody." I made my way to her office, knocked on the door then entered. She was yelling at someone on the phone, *I would hate to be that person.* "What the fuck do you want?" she looked over at me, "calm down man, I'm on your side," "I just want things to be perfect, this is my life and career on the line, so don't tell me to calm down," "it's to late for that...you have people in your office thinking that they did something wrong and your working yourself up...Billie," "I just have so much to do, I don't know what I am going to do." I watched her pace back and forth and I kept trying to get her attention, eventually I just grabbed her and kissed her. She paused and looked at me with her mouth open, "I could of hit you, but I didn't want you to have a mark on your face, everything is going to work out perfectly Billie...you got this," I stood looking at her, as she slowly made her way to her desk and sat down, "I'm still tryin to wrap my mind around the fact that you kissed me," "it got your attention didn't it," I started laughing, "you're right Adrian, I got this." I walked out of the office and helped put the final touches on the show.

The show kicked off on time, and there were so many people artist there that I couldn't believe my eyes. I walked around with Billie as she worked the room and talked with some of her people from New York, I drifted around the room slowly catching eyes with various women that caught my eye. Of course I flirted with them, I couldn't help myself. In no time I spotted Dr. Charal walking around and admiring the art work, I made my way over to her and started talking to her. She said that she wanted to go somewhere private, so I took her into one of the offices. "So, whats up?" she said nothing back, just sat me down in the chair, "I guess you were cool with the kiss?" she kissing me, as she pulled off my clothes and started sucking on my neck and biting me. I felt her move all around

94

my body, and I just laid my head back, as she went to work on me.

30 mins later I walked out the room feeling good and trying to gather my thoughts, I quickly ran into the bathroom as well to get my freshness back. "Can everyone gather around the stage please," I heard Roslyn's voice over the speakers, I stood there right along with the crowd. "I want to thank you for coming out tonight, this has been an amazing first showcase in LA and we do hope that you all come back again." Everyone clapped and went back to talking amongst each other, said there goodbyes, and some even bought a few paintings.

I had been clean for about three years now, time just seemed to take me away because I was busy with Isaac, working with Billie and going to school. I even saw Natasha a few times during my healing process, it seemed like each and everyday we were becoming those two kids who went to sleep outside, only to rise with the sun and go running. She even spent the night a few times, and I loved having her in my arms again. Although her fiancée still has no idea whats going on, hell neither do I and I'm doing it.

"Yo Adrian," I heard Billie yell my name from across the room, I gave her the head nod to let her know that she had my ears, "we need more ice, I'm to fucked up to drive," we both started laughin, I waved her off to let her know that I got it. I grabbed the car keys to the Rover off of the table and made my way to the store, I almost jumped out my pants when I felt my phone vibrating. "Hello," "what up girl? I hope you don't think that I forgot about you," "who is this?" "Swift," "oh man whats up, how have you been?" "Pretty good, I know that its been a long time since we talked but I have been working with my friend on some projects and we have been looking into what happened to you and your mom," "did you find anything?" "I'm going to come by in a few days to talk to you about it," "ok man, talk to you later," "peace." I never even thought about that until now, I parked the car, went inside the store and got some ice. *My mom had been gone for about 5 years now and I still haven't been to her grave and to top it off I am about to find out some things that never even crossed my mind.* I opened up the trunk of the car, placed the bags of ice in there and closed it. "Adrian," I turned around, "what up homie, you remember me," "not really," "you got into a fight with me and some of my people," "oh and you fired off the gun," "yea, and you busted me in my head with one." I started to step back, letting him know that I didn't want any problems, "dude that was three years ago," "I can never forget havin a female crack my head open," "I don't know what to tell you man I'm over it, I don't even fuck with Kirk no more," "that's not the way he putting it out there," he and two of his boys kept moving toward me, I guess I was going to have to be the person in a tank full of sharks. I felt his hand go across my face, I hit him back and we started fighting right there in the parking lot, I heard people yelling stop, and trying to pull them off of me, but no one wanted to go near a dude with a gun. My head got slammed through the back window, as I fell to the ground I felt his foot ram into my ribs and stomach, then I felt my head bounce off of the pavement…twice. He took my face into his hand, "look at me bitch," I couldn't even see his face with the blood dripping down my eyes, "you tell that nigga Kirk that I'm coming for him," his knee connected with my face…my head flew back as blood came out of my mouth and my head landed on the concrete.

I laid there with my eyes wide open, feeling my blood spill from my body, I felt like I was dying, that everything started to move in slow motion. Every breath hurt me more and more, the tears that came from my eyes didn't make me feel any better. People gathered around me, trying to keep me awake and talking to me, "miss my name is Danny, and I'm a doctor, I am going to go threw your pockets to find your identification, I have my wife calling you an ambulance, I am going to do the best that I can until they get here," everything that he was saying was going in and out. I started to stare into the bright light that had entered my line of sight, I continued to walk toward it and as I did I felt my breathing get fainter. I took my last breath, *I started running toward a figure that resembled my mother but it seemed like I could never reach her, I kept going and going holding my hand out to her, crying out for her…I placed my hand over my heart as I felt a slight jolt, then I fell to the ground as I felt another one enter my body like electricity.* "Adrian stay with me, we are almost to the hospital," said the EMT as he checked my eyes.

I was really hoping that I had got wasted at the party, passed out, and this was all just a bad dream. But the pain that I felt in my body, listening to my heartbeat, let me know just how fucked up I really was. It was obvious that I had major head injury, maybe a few broken ribs. But I wouldn't fully know anything until the doctor came to talk to me. I took a few breathes and tried to speak. "Don't even try to talk, the doctor said that it would be painful…you have two broken and bruised ribs, you had to have surgery twice," I closed my eyes as she continued to talk to me, "why are you here?" "I wanted to be the first person that you saw when you woke up," "Natasha, I…" "I know Adrian." She gently kissed me on my forehead and walked out of the room. A few hours later Billie, Roslyn and my doctor walked into the room. Everything that he was informing me about, I had already heard, and then the room grew silent as if someone had just died. The doctor had told me something that was going to change my life forever.

3 days later…I was back at home watching Isaac play and continue to grow into a handsome young man. It must be great to be a child, and not have to deal with all the problems that the world puts on you. And part of you wishes that you can go back to that time, and for maybe a day not have to put up with the bullshit that life has to offer. I guess that in some way you could say that life was so much sweeter when you were younger. You didn't have to worry about rent, buying clothes, paying bills, and all that other stuff. But then, how would you ever grow and learn how to deal with the difficulties that life has to offer unless you experience and learn.

I sat in the chair in the den holding my head, not even moving an inch. "How you feelin?" Billie asked as she stood in the doorway, "I can't take anything for the pain, it hurts like hell everytime my body moves a certain way…if I would of never did drugs, I wouldn't be in this position," "everybody makes mistakes, that's how we learn," "oh yea, how many people do you know loose there mother, has an aunt who hates them, finds out there dad was fucking cheater and dies on the same day, has to raise a little brother, and spends the last four plus years blaming themselves for there mothers death…" "and lets not forget Natasha leaving you again for another woman, getting engaged to her and yet still finds the time to continue to love you," "Billie…" "Adrian, I know what the doctor said, and you're life isn't over yet, you still have time." I sat there staring at her, I knew that she was right in what she was saying. I slowly stood up from the chair, "do you need help?" "I can manage," I moved the tray and made my way toward Billie, "the hard part is over now, its time to heal," Billie handed me the car keys.

I sat there taping my fingers on the steering wheel, I couldn't believe that I had been sitting there for 10 minutes and didn't even make a move…I wiped my hand across my face…I got out of the car and made my way over to my mother's grave. Every step I took made me more emotional, I had flashes of her in my head of the last time we had talked and I saw her face. I stopped in front of her grave, I felt like I was about to give a speech in front of thousands of people. "I'm sorry it took me so long to come and see you, I felt like everyone was against me and I had no way out. I was told so many times that it was my fault that you died, that I believed it myself, and it is my fault, if I never would of missed my curfew you would be alive today. I miss you so much, I would give anything just to see your face again, to hug you, or watch our shows like we used to do. I love you mom, and from this point on I am going to make you proud." I bowed my head as the tears fell from my eyes. I placed my fingers to my lips, in then to my mother's grave. I turned around and walked away. As I took one last look, I saw her standing there smiling at me and then she disappeared.

Later that night, I laid in my bed with the lights dimmed low, my mind was playing my thoughts like they were a never ending movie. I just wanted them to stop; I just wanted my mind to take a break for once. "Adrian you have a visitor," said Roslyn knocking on my door. I got myself to my feet just as Natasha had walked in, "you didn't have to get up," "I'm fine, what brings you here?" "It's over between me and my fiancée, it ended a few days ago," "oh, I'm sorry," "no your not…my heart never left you, and she didn't love me, abuse isn't love," "very true." Natasha got up and walked toward me, she placed her hand on the side of my face, "Adrian I…" "I know," my lips met hers as we shared a passionate kiss, her arms wrapped around my body and I immediately felt the pain, "we can't do this, you're still in pain," "the love that I feel for you, out weights the pain that I feel," "you just want some of my goodies," "no, I just want to embed your beauty into my memories before my eyesight completely fails me," "what?" what are you talking about?" "I'm losing my sight, the damage that was done affected me in a way that couldn't be seen," "then I have a lot to show you before you go blind." I watched as she slowly took off her clothes, and made her way toward me. She undressed me and threw my clothes on the floor along with hers. My hands moved up and down her body, I laid her down on the bed and got on top of her, kissing every inch of her body as I made my way down. Licking and sucking on her breast as I caressed each one, letting my tongue slide across her stomach, until I reached her jewel. I parted her lips with my tongue, as I dove in licking and sucking every part of her, playing on her spot as she begins to moan a little louder. All I wanted to do was make love to her all night, to make her cum as many times as her body would allow, and that's exactly what I did.

I woke up the next morning feeling the pain move over my body, for about 5 minutes I just laid there not even moving. *This shit is crazy.* I looked over my shoulder to find Natasha sleeping peacefully, I got out of the bed as quietly as I could and went to use the bathroom. I turned on the shower and looked at the scare that I had on my body. "Let me in Adrian," I unlocked the door for Natasha, "do you need some help?" "just cut the back," she took the scissors and cut my bandage, there was so much blood, that I knew it was going to hurt like hell when I pulled it off. "Wait…why don't we get in the shower, let the water hit it and slowly pull it off?" "Ok love." We both jumped into the shower, and slowly removed the bandage; the pain was a little less compared to what it could have been.

After we had got out of the shower, we walked back into the bedroom and dried off. I got half way dressed and then sat down in the chair. I watched Natasha as she was getting dressed; you could see the bruises that were on her body, there were some on her thighs, her lower back, and back of her leg. *I wish I could just fuck that girl up one more time, just to make her bleed, ugh I know that she isn't worth it though.* I grabbed Natasha by the wrist as I snapped back into reality, "my pain is your pain," I said, I pulled her toward me and started kissing her, she sat down on my lap, as my hands moved up and down her body. "Hey you two, breakfast is ready," said Roslyn knocking on the door, "be out in a minute," I yelled. I stole one more kiss, then Natasha got off of me, "you should really let that breathe," "ok baby," I put on my sports bra, "I will put on a tank top if we go anywhere," "if we go anywhere." We both smiled.

We all sat down at a table full of food, I hadn't had breakfast like this since my mom would throw down in the kitchen. Everything I learned, I learned from her, and she continues to teach me even in her death. "Hi Isaac," "Adrian...I miss you," "I missed you too," I kissed him on the cheek, "did the doctor fix you?" "Yes, but I'm still hurting," "where?" "Right here," I pointed to my ribs and showed him the stitches, "can I touch it?" "No...eat your food." We all started eating and talking about everything that had been going on, in the back of my mind I kept thinking about how I was going to tell Isaac that I was losing my eyesight. "What's wrong?" I looked over at Isaac, "you look sad," everyone at the table got quiet, "I have to talk you about something, and you may not understand it right now," "is it bad?" "I don't know," "are you going to die like daddy did?" "No, I'm never going to leave you little man," "whats wrong?" "I am going blind," he sat there staring at me for a good second, "like Ray?" "Yea, like Ray." He didn't say anything else, he just went back to eating his food and so did we.

I sat outside watching Isaac play with the next door neighbor's kid, and every now and then he would look over at me and smile. "So, please tell me that you and Natasha hooked up," "we fucked," "I mean, you two are a couple," I

100

looked over at Natasha, "are we a couple?" "I don't know, are we?" "You two piss me off," "we're not dating," "why not?" "Yall should be married by now, shit," "Natasha," "yes baby," "will you go out with me now?" "Yes." She leaned over and kissed me. "Now yall make me sick," Billie got up and walked back into the house.

The air felt so good on my skin, there wasn't even any pain to complain about, it felt great…20 minutes later…a white Audi pulled up in front of the house, we kept looking like who the fuck is that, and then when he turned around I saw that it was Swift. He came up the steps and hugged me; I introduced him to my girl. "Hey, anything you have to tell me, you can say in front of them, so don't beat around the bush," "we found out who raped you," "who was it?" "It was Kirk," "why doesn't that surprise me?" "I know that you trusted him," "we weren't really friends to begin with," I rubbed the back of my neck, "we found out who the hit and run driver was in your accident?" "Damn man, can't you tell me some good news?" "You said don't beat around the bush, so I'm laying it out for you," "who's the bastard that killed my mom," "Kirk." My eyes moved on him quickly, and I replayed what he said in my head, "his blood was on the steering wheel, it matched," "Kirk…fuckin Kirk." I got up from my chair, and started yelling and screaming like a mad woman, until I finally sat down on the stairs and cried. I felt Isaac wrap his arms around my head, "are you ok?" "I'm ok, go play," "I love you Adrian," "I love you more." I went into the house, put on my shoes, and a jacket, walked back out the house, "he is going to pay…take me to Jamal's house," "Are you crazy?" "Kirk shot his little brother because he was stealing from him, I helped him get rid of the body, now are you going to take me or am I going to take myself?"

We drove to Jamal's house not having much of a conversation; I just stared out the window looking at all the things that I wasn't going to see anymore. We pulled up into the driveway and got out the car. "What the fuck are you doing here?" "I want to talk to Jamal," "get the fuck out of here," "Jamal," I started yelling, "Jamal," I saw him stand in the doorway, "Adrian? You got a lot of nerve comin to my place," "I want to show you something, and then I want you to do something for me," "why should I trust you?" "Because I know where your brother is and I know who did it." We got back into the car, and he followed us to where the body was dumped. We stood around it as he had his boys dig up his body…once they hit the box, they pulled it out, broke it open, and Jamal just stood there staring at the skeleton that his brother had become, I never thought that I would see him cry.

"Talk to me Adrian, what the fuck happened?" "Kirk was arguing with your brother, saying that he was stealing from him for years. And then Kirk just snapped and shot him, when I came in he went a little crazy on me," "you already know that I am going to kill him, what do you want from me?" "I want you to make him suffer…he raped me and he was the hit and run driver that killed my mom…I want him to suffer for the rest of his life because killing him is given him the easy way out," "I want him dead," "and I want him to suffer," "he killed your mom, he stole your virginity," "and then he took my sight…in less then a few weeks I am going to go blind because of some shit that went down when I was with him…now all I want to do is hear him cry out in pain and cry in agony until he begs you to take his life, and all you do is walk away," "for you Adrian, I will do that."

A few hours later we pulled up to Kirk's house, I haven't seen him since the day I went into the hospital for being on that damn drug that he gave me. Jamal's boys covered the back of the house, and we went to the front door, and walked inside. Kirk was sitting on the couch getting ready to blaze, "long time no see nigga, where you been hidin?" "I've been getting clean," "you don't know what you're missing," "I'm not missing a damn thing," "then why you here," "I'm giving you a chance to confess what you did to me," "I didn't do shit to you," "oh ok, so your seamen just happened to be found between my legs," "you wanted it," "I was so fuckin high that I couldn't even keep my eyes open," "I've done worst," "oh yea like what," "I had a hit and run, some bitch and her kid, I ran from the scene because I was so fucked up that I would have been locked up for sure," "that bitch that you killed happened to be my mother, and that child was me." He looked up at me, "look man, I apologize for what I did to you and killin your mom…we cool?" he stood up and held out his hand, I grabbed it, "we are never going to be cool," I pulled him across the table and slammed his against the wall and let Jamal and his boys take over. They dragged him outside, and started beating the shit out of him, I just watched, "you know you want some of this Adrian," "I'm good Jamal, just make him suffer," I walked toward the car with Swift, we both got inside and then he peeled off. "Thanks Swift," "anything for you."

Back at home, I went inside, kissed my baby brother, and then went into my room. Natasha sat there looking at me; I threw my jacket on the desk, kicked off my shoes, took off my jeans and got into bed with her. I buried my face into her arms as she held me tight. "Do you want to get married?" "What?" "Do you want to get married?" "Where is this comin from Adrian?" "I was just thinking that if you wanted to get married then we should do it now, so that I could see you in your dress," she got off the bed, opened up her jewelry box, pulled something out and then got back in the bed. "When we were younger you gave me this ring, you saved up all your money just so that you could get it for me," I watched as she put it on her ring finger, "we never said that we would get married but that we would make each other a promise," "to always love each other no matter what," "and I think we have been threw enough bullshit to say that we have." She handed me the other ring that I told her to hold, she took my hand and placed it on there. "I love you Adrian," "I love you too Natasha," we kissed each other and then went to sleep.

I was feeling so weak that I couldn't even get off the bed; I just laid there staring at the wall, not thinking about anything. I wanted to get up and run around, I just didn't want to lay here and sleep, but I felt like that was all that I could do. Every week my sight begins to fail me more and more, and the doctor said that in a matter of time my vision would be completely gone. I went into a temporary state of depression, I was going threw so many emotions, I was going to lose my vision, I was going to be blind for the rest of my life. And I couldn't do shit.

Each and everyday I would start to train my myself to trust my instincts when it came to movin in the dark, I would walk around with my eyes closed so that I can begin to feel my surroundings. After a while I started to get pretty good at it because I wasn't about to let this be my downfall. "Adrian come here for a second," said Billie, I made my way over to her studio that she had built in her house, "I want you to take a look at my new collection," "you never show anyone before the show," "I have to make an exception in your case, because the doctor called today," "and?" "You're gonna lose your vision completely before the week is out," "it was going to happen sooner or later," "I'm sorry man," "don't be…I have learned that with every action comes a consequence, whether it is good or bad, if I never would of hung out with Kirk I never would have been in a fight, and it never would of came back to bite me in the ass, hell I wouldn't have even done drugs, but shit happens," "we also learn from our mistakes and can teach others," "this isn't going to destroy me," "that's because you're a damn fighter," "but your paintings are beautiful man, people are going to love it," "thanks bro."

My days were filled with walking Isaac to school, seeing everyone joke and play, visiting my grandma when I got the chance. And walking around the city, so that I can get used to the sounds, smells, and the environment around me, I liked the idea that my other senses would become more enhanced and sharper…30 minutes later, I stood in front of Natasha's office, I went inside to go and visit her, thinking that maybe we could do lunch or something. She worked as a computer engineer at her grandfathers company, eventually she was going to be able to run this place. I took the elevator up to the tenth floor; I had never really been in here before. I found her secretary and talked to her for a little bit because Natasha was having a conference call.

"You can go in now Adrian," "thank you," I walked into her office and sat down in the chair across from her. "Looks like someone could use a drink," "that sounds good right about now," "maybe when you get home later," "yea maybe…how did you get here?" "I walked," "what? You can't walk around the streets of LA like that, are you crazy?" "I can't just sit at home all day, drowning in my sorrows, and then going to work, and then coming back home, it's boring," "it's safe, what if something happened to you?" "You know how they say there is no progress without risk, well I am taken a risk every time I step out my door so that I can make progress, I don't want this to be a handicap that plays against me. I want to own it and dominate it," I got up from the chair and headed for the door, "Adrian wait…I just don't like the idea of losing you again, I mean shit, you've been in the hospital about 3 times in your life now, and I just don't want something to catch up to you again," she stood in front of me with her arms around my neck, "don't look at me like that," "like what?" "Baby you gotta work," "I don't care."

She pulled me by my shirt over to her desk, she sat down and pulled me between her legs, "besides I know that you can't resist me in a skirt," she licked her lips and pulled me into kiss her. I moved her a little more to the edge of her desk, as I made my way between her legs, pulling off her panties, I pulled her skirt up, and started to treat myself to her pussy, her hands grabbing the back of my neck and my hair. *I hate quickies*. I fucked my baby the way that she liked it when we had moments like this; I pushed deep inside of her, fucked fucking her slowly, until she came into my mouth and all over her desk.

I left her office smiling as I made my way back to Isaac's school to pick him up, *damn time flies by when you're having fun*. I sat there on the step's waiting for him to come out, a few minutes later he came out smiling and running toward me, he jumped into my arms. "Can we get some ice cream?" "Not before dinner," "please," "one scoop, and then you can eat the rest after dinner, deal?" "Deal." We made our way to the ice cream parlor, and then went back home to munch on some of it before everyone got home.

There was one last thing that I wanted to do before my vision had left me, I wanted to ride my motorcycle threw the streets and feel the wind on my face, feel the adrenaline build up inside of me. "I know that you are not thinking what I think you are," said Roslyn standing next to me, "this is what I live for," "Billie always said that you loved to live life in the fast lane and in the outdoors," "do you want to ride?" "I am not to excited about motorcycles, I like to be secured all around," "I will keep you safe, just trust me, we will go around the block a few times," "just a few times," "five minutes of your life," "damn it Adrian, if I get hurt," "I wont let nothing happen to you." We both put on helmets, I jumped on the bike, and Roslyn got on behind me, she wrapped her arms around me tight, *keep us safe mom*. I started up the bike, and pulled out of the garage and driveway, I started to take it easy for a bit, *don't be scared, and just push it*. I started to ride the bike like I was racing on a track going around the block a few times like I said I would, we stopped when we saw Natasha and Billie pull into the yard. "Oh hell yea, let me get my shit so that we can roll out to the beach before the sun set," said Billie running up the driveway, "I guess I will change and tag along." Roslyn jumped off the bike, and I did the same, "that was so fuckin amazing, ugh I felt so free," "my mom introduced me to motorcycles, I could remember being a kid and she would take me around the neighborhood a few times and as I got older and was able to hold on to her, she would go faster and faster, moving threw traffic, I fell in love with it, by the time I turned 13 she was teaching how to drive them and fix them, everything," "she sounds like an amazing woman, I wish I would have had the chance to meet her," "she knows who you are, and I am sure that she likes you." I glanced up at the sky.

We asked our neighbor to watch Isaac as we made our way to the beach on our motorcycles; once we arrived we sat there in the sand with our girls and watched as the sun went down. *There were so many things that I wasn't going to be able to see anymore, so many things that I would have to just remember by memory, I was as much prepared as I was sacred to face what was coming.* After a few hours, we made our way back home, had dinner and spent the rest of the night watching movies and enjoying each others company.

Three days later, I woke up in darkness, my vision was now completely gone and I had been dealing with it for about two days now. It was time for me to get dressed and ready for Billie's show tonight, I know that there was only so much that I could do but I was determined to help. I sat there in the gallery listening to everything that was going on around me, "you need to relax Billie," "how the hell did you know I was sitting here?" "I have powers," "shut up," "they are going to love it, you are an amazing artist," "I just hope that they see what I see," "that's why you explain it to them, so that they can see what you see," "ugh, I need a drink," "no you don't, you need to breath because in a few hours it is going to kick off and you are going to reveal your new collection."

Everyone clapped as Billie took the stage and thanked everyone for coming, "tonight I want to introduce my collection, before I reveal it I want to give you the story behind it. This collection is dedicated to my bestfriend and little sister Adrian Coolidge, I have known her all my life and I have watched her grow and make so many mistakes. And when she was sixteen she was in a car accident, she lost her mother, she lost the woman that she loved, and was hated by her own family. Her path became filled with so much darkness, her life became about drugs and making money. This lead to her being hurt in so many ways that you couldn't even imagine, I never left her side, I helped her as much as she would let me until she was able to push herself. Now at the age of 21, she stands before you blind because her actions caught up with her. I've never seen her give up, get depressed or not own up to it. Adrian inspired me to venture out and create something that I have never done before. I told her story threw my eyes and captured her pain. And because of her I feel like I have grown as a better artist and as a person because watching what she went threw and seeing her make it out alive and still carry the same strength, lets me know that I have no excuses as to why I am fucking up or not doing things the right way…with this being said, I present to you, Failure is Not an Option." Billie pulled the sheet off of her paintings, and everyone begin to clap and admire her work. I stood there staring up at the stage smiling because I knew that she was looking right at me.

In The End...

I had become someone that a lot of people could relate to,
I knew what it was like to lose someone that you love,
I knew what it was like to lose a mother,
I knew what it was like to have people blame you for
something that happened,
I knew what it was like to do drugs,
I knew what it was like to be raped,
I knew what it was like to get into a fight and then get shot
because the person had a problem with getting beat up by a
girl,
I knew what it was like to fight with your father because he
blamed you for the death of his wife,
I knew what it was like to almost die the same night because
the pain got the best of you and all you wanted to do was not
care anymore,
I knew what it was like to watch my baby brother hold my
drugs in his hand and almost take them because I was being
careless,
Then I found a way to get better with the help of a friend that
never left my side,
I found out that my father was cheating on my mother and
then in the same day he passed away,
I knew what it was like to have something come back and hunt
you,

And return I got the love of my life back and we built a future together,
And most importantly,
I have learned that even though part of me is gone,
It is not missing,
Because as long as I continue to push myself to do better,
And to be better then what I am,
Then there isn't a damn thing that can stop me from pursuing my dreams,
Because as long as I take risks,
I will always make progress.
My name is Adrian Coolidge, and this was my story…

The Diary of Death Row

Day 1: March 28, 2008

Has a scent ever caught your senses when you were just walking around? Like food that reminds you of your moms or grandmas cooking and it just makes you smile...what about the taste you get after kissing your girl or guy, and you taste there lip gloss or chapstick along with their lips, and it tastes like strawberries...and what about sitting around with your friends, and you just start laughing because you thought of something funny and everyone is looking at you like what the fuck? I love that...memories are all we have when it comes to certain things or people...then love enters your life, and not just any kind of love, I'm talking about that kind that goes pass your heart and straight into your soul. And the one thing you never forget about that person when it has ended was the little things they did for you. I love having that feeling.

In any case you can't have the good without the bad or the love without the hate. So let me ask you this, do you know what it's like to smell fire burning? I'm sure you said yes, and you can tell the difference between a blaze of a forest fire, and cooking BBQ in your backyard...*damn I love me some ribs, I haven't had that in a minute, hell even a steak would be nice*...any who, have you ever seen those shows with people who set themselves on fire just to see how long they can stay that way…personally I wouldn't be caught dead doing that shit…on the other hand have you seen a man on fire? Not the movie, but an actual person, right in front of your eyes, and you can smell their flesh burning and see it at the same time? I only wish that I could answer no the way some of you just did in your mind. My memories won't free me from it, my eyes won't hide it, my dreams continue to show it, and the smell just makes me sick to my stomach. So I hate everything about fires, it brings back everything I want to forget.

Day 19: April 15, 2008

You know how almost every family has their secrets and when you ask a certain question you get an answer, but when you ask another person you get a different story? I hate that, but I like how someone pulls you to the side and keeps it real with you and just lays out nothing but the truth…that's what I am going to do for you, I am going to tell you the truth about my life, I am not going to sugar coat it, it will not be censored, I just want to be able to tell you how deep my pain goes…my name is Deavin Janice Hunt, I was born June 27, 1987 in Riverside, California. My current leaving address is the California Institute for Women, there are a lot of rules here, and the guards have warmed up to me. I didn't think they could be that nice, I assume that it's because I am 19 years old and on death row.

Day 24: April 20, 2008

My mom and dad were married for some years, but on October 1991 my parents split up. He took my brother Memphis and left me and my sister Lily. *I saw Memphis three times after that, and now he is some big time author in New York.* I was four at the time and my sister was two. My mom did just fine without him, she worked as an international marketing manager, and sometimes they would have her travel. The following year my mom met a man named Clyde, he was dark chocolate, brown eyes, faded haircut, and a nice smile. Clyde was a nice man and he was good to my mom. By the end of the year, he had moved into our home, my mom was so excited that he was there too…three years later my mom and Clyde got married in March of '95, I was eight and my sister six. We never called him dad, well at least I didn't.

"Go get dressed," Clyde said to us, we got ready, got into the car and he drove us to Moreno Valley. "Put this on," he handed us some clothes to change into, "why?" I asked, "Because I told you too." We changed in the backseat of the car, he pulled over, "get out," we got out the car…he had us stand on the corner and ask people for money. Within thirty-minutes we had twenty dollars, after being out there for five hours we had eighty dollars. I took my sister by the hand and we started walking home, I know that it was a thirty-minute drive, so walking would take forever. We walked a good three miles and then Clyde picked us up, had us change, and took us home. "How much did you make?" I handed him the money, "good work girls, now I want this to stay between me and you." He got up and started cooking before my mom got home. "Why did he make us do that?" my sister asked me, "maybe he needs money," "doesn't he work," "yes." Clyde worked on computers and he made good money, I didn't get why he needed more. We all sat down and had dinner that night; no one spoke about what happened.

When November came around he had us out there almost every other day. And I will never forget the first time he beat us with a belt because we were short some money. Clyde didn't want us to bring back less then seventy dollars. We couldn't always make it, so we got beat, and we never got hit in the face. Before we could even talk to our mom, Clyde would tell her that we had an accident at the park and that is why we had bruises on our arms…one night I got up to use the bathroom, I heard my sister weeping a little bit, "Deavin is that you?" my mom called out from down stairs, "yea," "go check on your sister," "ok." I walked into the room and saw Clyde touching her, he looked over at me, and grabbed me before I could run out the door. He pushed me against the wall, "if you tell anyone about this I will kill your mother and sister," I stood there tryin not to cry, as soon as he left my sister ran and hugged me, I sat on the floor rocking her to sleep.

In December, I decided to start taking money, I became a hustler, what we got from people I would pocket some of what we made and I promised my sister that we wouldn't get beat ever again because we're never going to give him nothing less then what he wanted. I was determined to be my sister's angel and protect her from the evil that lived in our house.

Before we knew it, it was April of next year; I heard my mom and Clyde arguing in the kitchen. I watched as he pushed her into the counter and then slapped her across the face. He took a duffle bag and packed his clothes, shoes, underwear, everything he needed. My mom stopped him before he walked out the door, and begged him to stay. He dropped his bag, went into there room and they had make-up sex…the next day my mom had to go out of state on business, my sister was crying so hard because she wanted to go with her, I just stood there letting the tears come down my face…later that night, I wake up on the couch, I look around and I didn't see anyone, I walk to my sister's room and Clyde is on top of her, I grabbed a belt and hit him with it as hard as I could, I pulled my sister from underneath him, "go in my room and hide," Clyde grabbed me and slammed me face first on to the bed, I kept struggling, my pants were moved down to my ankles, I felt his hand on my pussy, then I saw him lick his fingers, he placed it inside of me, "I am going to teach you not to ever put hands on me again," I felt his hand more around my ass, as he spread my cheeks, he pushed his finger into my hole to open it up, then he slid his dick inside of me, and started pounding my little frame. All the tears and cries for help couldn't save me now. When he was done he took me to the bathroom and washed me off, he then carried me to my bed and went to wash my sister's sheets, as she laid in bed with me.

Day 26: April 22, 2008

Telling that story really took a lot out of me, I forgot that as kids sometimes we choose to forget things that have happened to us and then it ends up affecting us as we get older. The day I saved my sister from a future of pain, I sacrificed not only myself but my body for her. And I would do it all over again in a heartbeat, because I will be damned if I let someone take my sister's innocence away like that…I can't really write much more, my emotions are high and my energy is low.

Day 35: May 1, 2008

Nothing happened all next year, and not even the first few months of the following year. In May of '97 I saw Clyde spending more and more time with another woman, I couldn't believe that he was cheating on my mom who he said was the love of his life. He had asked me to keep his secret, and in return he would stay away from my sister, I couldn't help but to agree to that. When August came around my mom had to go on another trip again…on occasions when he wasn't with his new woman he would come into my room at night and get into bed with me. He would hold me and tell me how much I meant to him…on other nights, I would brace myself for whatever was about to happen…he moved me on to my back, pulled off my pjs and undies, licked his finger and started rubbing my pussy, "don't you like that," I shook my head no, he moved from the side of me and I watched as he started to undress himself, then his phone started ringing "hello," "hey baby, hows your trip?" "That's great; I am just making sure the kids are in bed now," "I love you too," "goodnight." He stood there looking at me, and then walked out of my room…I wish that you could of seen the smile on my face…when my mom came back home, I hugged her tight and told her thank you for everything, she just looked at me confused and told me and my sister that we meant the world to her…if she only knew what kind of man she had brought into our home, she would be able to see that our world was crashing down.

Day 39: May 5, 2008

I lay on my bed in my cell, as a tear comes from my eyes, I start thinking about how I would listen to rock music to make

116

me feel better, but I cant do that in here. I loved listening to Staind, I hope you know who they are, my songs were "reality" and "its been awhile" I could hear it now in my head, and I smile...all I can do now is let this ink bleed from my pen to my paper and write down the thoughts in my mind, from poetry to stories, each one has there own glory...there was a knock on my door, "yes," "I have to turn your light off soon," "I know," "what are you working on?" "a story of my life," "what are you going to name it?" "I have no clue," "I will give you five more minutes," "thanks CO," "I told you already, call me Lucky." Lucky is the only friend I really have in lock up, considering that death row inmates are segregated from each other, all I know about Lucky is that she is from North Carolina, a kick ass female, and she writes just like I do. I am looking forward to reading some of her work whenever she brings it to me. I hear a tap on the door, I have to go now.

Day 59: May 25, 2008

Three years had gone by and nothing happened, but each time he would tell me that he loves me and can't wait to hold me close to his body. Every time I braced myself for it to happen, nothing did. July 2000, I am now 13 years old, while I was taking a shower I had a feeling that something was going to happen, but quickly changed my mind because my mom was at home. When I got out the shower, I dried off my body, wrapped my towel around me, and opened the door. Clyde was standing there, he pushed me back into the bathroom, I called out for my mom, "she's not here," he said to me. I was pushed into the sink, my towel came off of me, and Clyde slid himself inside of me, he fucked me hard and long until he got what he wanted. As time moved on, I found that he was becoming more into me and wanting to have sex with me.

January 2001, I am 14 years old now, I make my way to the park and sit under a tree, my sunglasses hide the tears that live in my eyes, I am sick of all the bullshit, of not being able to tell anyone just because he would kill my mother and sister. I called for my dad, more then twice at this point and he has yet to return my phone call…I pull a knife out of my pocket, I place the blade up to my wrist, and out of nowhere someone grabs the hand that is holding the knife, "do you know that the most authentic thing about us is our capacity to create, to overcome, to endure, to transform, to love and to be greater then our suffering," she said to me, I looked up and locked eyes with her. Golden brown they were, her smile as beautiful as anything I had ever seen, her skin was a shade of brown, and she had long black hair. "Can you let me go?" I said to her, "can you talk to me?" I just stared at her, "if you don't like where the convo goes afterwards I will let you do what you were going to do," "why should I?" "Because I want you to take a chance on me." Her words were filled with so much sincerity, I let her take the knife from my hand and stood to my feet, we started walking around the park. "My name is Deavin," "I know who you are, we go to the same school, I always see you around," "really? I don't think I have ever seen you," "you always seem to be zoned out," "I tend to do that a lot…Are you going to tell me your name?" "It depends, on if you decide to live or die" she looked at me and smiled, "that's fair enough," "so, do you have a girlfriend?" "no," "have you ever had a girlfriend?" "no, I was never really big on relationships, I always seemed to push myself away from people, so I saw no point in trying," "then who is Lily?" I looked up at her, "I saw her name on your folder one day," "that's my baby sister, she means so much to me," "then why would you kill yourself, and leave her alone." I didn't think about Lily until now, I was so wrapped up in myself…when it started to get dark, I decided to live, she told me that her name was Mya and gave me her number.

Day 68: June 3, 2008

March 2002, Clyde didn't like Mya you can tell by the way he looked at her when she came over or when I would hug her. I thought it was the greatest thing in the world, I had found my happiness and it pissed him off…I had went over to her house as well, her family was nice and loving, I enjoyed being at there house…I couldn't believe how big her house was, I looked at pictures that she had on her dresser as I walked around her room, "that's my mom, she died two years ago, my dad gave me the bigger room because I am the only girl and he didn't want to be in here alone," "how did she die?" "A drunk driver hit her car, he lived and she died," she took the picture out of my hands and sat it back down. I looked at her and wiped the tear that had came out of her eye, she kissed me on my cheek and then my lips, "this stays between me and you," "of course," she looked at me waiting to hear what I said to say, I took a deep breath "your touch is gentle…I have never felt anything like that…I was raped and I still get raped till this day, and that was the only touch that I have ever known…I have always talked to girls, but never went any further," "I would never do anything to hurt you or cause you any kind of pain, we can go as slow as you want, all I ask is that you don't push me away." I placed my forehead on hers, leaned my head to the right and kissed her lips. We both smiled.

December 2002, I was laying in my bed texting Mya, we talked all day and night, Clyde had came into my room and I quickly put my phone down. "Whats going on with you in this girl?" he said to me pacing my room like a mad man, "nothing, we're just friends," "nothing more?" "no," "don't fuckin lie to me, you know that you are my girl, you belong to me." he came and sat down on my bed and started touching me, I moved away from him, he grabbed me and held me down as he got on top of me. "You kissed her didn't you, didn't you?" he yelled at me, "yes," I said back to him. He started to remove his clothes and mine, I just laid there lifeless as he slid himself inside of me, I felt him movin in and out of me, he seemed to be getting angry, "fuck," he yelled out, "act like you want it," I couldn't bring myself to do it because I didn't want it, "fuck this," he got off of me, turned me on to my stomach and struck my back three times, I screamed out, "oh now you want to scream," he

119

tried to get it from behind, pounding me like crazy, but was angry that he couldn't perform to his abilities.

Day 78: June 10, 2008

You know shit like this makes a person go crazy, but I am keeping my word and not sugar coating anything…I have realized that when it comes to me I would be facing my own demons all over again that comes from my past…and I have yet to hit the core of my problem, and yet I am stuck in deciding if I should warn you before time or just let it hit you the way that it did me.

Day 95: June 27, 2008

Today is my birthday, I am now 20 years old and spending it in jail. How great is that? The day just seemed to drag on, once I was back in my cell, it was everything all over again, I lay here waiting for my light to go off and then go right to sleep. "Hey Deavin you up?" I heard Lucky's voice, "yea," "come on get up, I have a surprise for you." the door opened and I stood there, I was taken to a phone, "happy birthday," Lucky said to me as I took the phone out of her hand. "hello," "it feels so good to hear your voice," my heart started to skip a beat, "Mya," "I miss you so much baby," "I miss you too," "I am sorry I wasn't there, happy birthday baby, I love you," "I love you too," I couldn't help but to smile and feel so much joy inside of me, "I went to visit your sister for you on your birthday," tears filled my eyes, "you didn't have to do that," "I wanted too, I love you DJ," "I love you so much more." We got off the phone, and I walked back to my cell happy as I can be, when I went into my room there was a box on my bed, I looked over at Lucky then back at the box, I opened it in there was a strawberry cake, a big smile cut across my face, I pulled out an envelope in there were pictures of my girl dressed in my clothes lookin sexy as hell…I split the cake up with the guards because I couldn't eat it all by myself. "Whats with the big smile?" Lucky asked me, "long story," "maybe I can read it in your book one day," "yea, maybe." I started laughing and ate the rest of my cake.

Day 103: July 5, 2008

The more time me and Mya spent together, the more I just wanted to be around her, she became like a part of me, the air that I breathed. Mya became someone that I didn't want to live without; I just bring myself to tell her that I love her, not having ever experienced it before. I talked to my mom about it, she just said "tell her how you feel, because she could feel the same way," I just kept going back and forth on it, but I knew that eventually it would come out. I sat there looking at her during lunch time; she would always glance back at me and smile, until she made her way over to me. People would wonder if we were dating but we never gave them an answer, we would just smile and look at each other. I knew that in my heart I was falling for her, I just didn't know if I would be able to ever tell her.

Day 108: July 10, 2008

July 20, 2003, I and Mya were out for a walk at the park, it seemed funny being there because it was the same place where she stopped me from making the biggest mistake of my life. I just looked over at her, "what? You have been in like another world all day," she said to me, "nothing, I just want to look at you," "yea sure," "no I mean," I stopped her from walking and looked into her eyes, "you mean so much to me, everytime I see you my heart begins to race and I feel like a little kid," "what are you saying DJ," "I want you to be my girlfriend," I looked up at her, "I would love nothing more then to be your girl."

Next Year

August 2004, Lily was getting ready to go to high school, I couldn't believe that she was already about to be 14 years old. I still had a year left, and Mya was starting her first year in college, she is a year older then me...I waited outside the school for my mom to pick me up, she was never late like this, when I saw her car pull up, I jumped in and looked over only to see Clyde's face. "Hey baby, bet you didn't expect to see me," "where's my mom?" "she got held up in a meeting and asked me to pick you up," "oh," "yea…so when were you going to tell me that you and Mya are a couple?" I just looked at him, "did you think it was going to stay a secret forever? I told you that you belong to me, along with your body," "she makes me happy," "no she doesn't, she is only with you because she feels sorry for you. I make you happy, everytime I touch you and kiss on you," "you don't make me happy the way that she does." Clyde looked over at me and I looked at him, the rest of the drive was quiet. I started to wonder what was going happen; I had a feeling that things were going to get worst before they got better.

October 1, 2004, I had just got done talking to Mya, I thought that I was in the house alone, for some reason I just had a break down and started crying in the corner, Clyde had said to me "no one will ever love me," that I was "nothing more then an easy little bitch that doesn't know how to keep her legs closed." I hated that he was trying to break me down, to make me do something that I would regret, my mom came into the living room, tears were in her eyes, "I heard everything," she said to me, and she kneeled down and held me in her arms. "What happened?" "I can't tell you," "you can tell me anything," "since I was 8 years old he raped me, after I protected Lily from getting raped, he never tried to touch her again after that, he only came after me. Everytime he told you that we hurt ourselves at the park or running around outside, was a lie, he beat us. I never said anything because he told me that he would kill you and Lily, I didn't want anything to happen to you guys." My mom just held me tight, she pulled out her phone and told two of her friends to come over, one of them changed all the locks on the door so that Clyde couldn't get in…we stayed in the house as my mom went outside, Clyde pulled up and got out the car, "whats going on?" my mom went up and slapped him across the face, he was about to hit my mom, but her friends grabbed him, pushed him into the car and started stomping on him like there was no tomorrow. Then they picked him up and threw him into the car, Clyde pulled out of the driveway and sped away.

Day 120: July 22, 2008

I can't believe that I am this far into my story; I thought that it would take longer then this to get everything out on paper. I just sit here in my cell, preparing myself to tell you what happens next, I lay back on my bed and look up at my ceiling and then over at the pictures of Mya. I would have truly married her and started a family with her, I guess some things are greater then others if you let it…my mind started to show flashes of that night, I just tried to shake it off…its time to let things hit you the way that it hit me.

Day 134: July 6, 2008

Thanksgiving…8:00am, I woke up feeling good; I got out of bed and looked out my window. The sky was cloudy, but by noon I knew that the sun would begin to shine. I could smell turkey and ham roaming all thru the house. I put on some sweat pants and made my way into the kitchen, where my mom and Lily were cooking. I started peeling the yams because I always made the pies and cakes, when we were almost done I went into my room and tried to find something to wear…I went and took a shower, got dressed, and went to join my family for dinner. Lily looked over at my mom and she nodded her head, Lily jumped up from the table and went down the hall, she came back with a box, "we got these for each of us," she opened a box that contained a ring, "it goes on your thumb, it represents our new bond that can not be broken by anyone," I put the ring on my hand, "oh and here wear this, this will make your outfit look better," she put a necklace around my neck that had a cross on it. We hugged and started to finish our dinner.

When 6:00pm came around, Mya had came to pick me up so that I can join her and her family for dinner. I was quiet the whole trip there, Mya held my hand, I guess she could tell that I was nervous. When we got to her house, she kissed me and said "everything is going to be fine, they are going to love you because I love you," I took a deeper breath then normal and followed her into the house…I met so many people that my head was spinning, around 7:30pm we all sat at the table and begin eating...her family was warm and loving, and they made me feel like I was apart of there family and they had just met me...Mya had me go with her to her room so that we could enjoy dessert alone, she sat down on the chair, and I sat between her legs with my back on her chest. She started feeding me strawberry cake...when it was gone, we laid there under the stars, Mya wrapped her arms around me and started kissing me on my neck, I looked up at her and she kissed me on my lips, it begin to get more intense with each touch. I got up from where I was sitting, the only time I had ever had sex was with Clyde...I held my head down, Mya lifted it up and kissed me gently, "I am not going to hurt you," I closed my eyes as her arms wrapped around my neck, and we begin kissing.

We made our way into her bedroom, my arms were lifted in the air, and my shirt pulled off my body along with my bra. I felt her lips on my skin as she laid me down on the bed. Her lips moved from my lips to my neck, I felt her sucking on me, as her tongue trailed down to my breast, she sucked and licked around my breast as she caressed it. Mya sat on top of me, pulled off her clothes and bra. I watched as she undressed me and then herself. I closed my eyes feeling her kissing on my thighs, her lips were so gentle as she kissed my pussy gently, I felt myself get wet, her tongue entered my lips, she begin to suck on my jewel and lick me up and down, hitting my spot each time. I bit on my bottom lip, as she began to lick harder, I pushed her head into my pussy wanting her to go deeper inside me, I put a pillow over my face so I wouldn't get to loud, my juices were screaming to be set free, as she sucked on my spot. My juices flowed out of me like a river. I felt her kissing back up my body. She moved the pillow, kissed me on my lips, "you taste so sweet," she said licking her lips. I smiled, pulled her down and kissed her. She moved back up, took my hand, placed my hand between her legs, she was so wet, "you see what you do to me DJ." Before I got a chance to do anything her dad started calling for us to come down...we made our way back downstairs with her family, 20 minutes later I got dropped off at home.

I walked into the house with a smile that could not be erased; I made my way into my sister's room, tucked her in, and kissed her on the forehead. Her eyes opened. "Are we going to watch All Dogs go to Heaven Christmas Carol tomorrow?" I started laughing, "of course," I said with a smile. She smiled and I left the room, I looked in on my mom and she was sound asleep. I went into my room, changed into shorts and a white beater; I got in bed and stared at the ceiling.

12:30am, I couldn't sleep for nothing, I pulled myself out of the bed and went to go get something to drink. While I made my way back to my room, I felt something hit me from behind...when I came to I was tied to a chair, across from me were my mom and sister. I looked up and saw Clyde, he was shaken his head and pacing as if something was wrong. "We had something good Deavin, why did you have to fuck it up?" he yelled as he removed the tape from my mouth, he started looking at my body, "what is this shit on your neck, on your body," his eyes burned into me, "answer me," he hit me across the face, "you fucked her didn't you?" it was hard not to smile because I started thinking about Mya and how we had just made love. "You think this shit is funny? I told you, you belong to me," "I don't belong to anybody." He pulled out a knife and cut me from the chair, "you think she better then me, you think you can just giver yourself to someone." My clothes were pulled from my body, I felt him enter me from behind, he pulled my hair back, "she will never be able to fuck you like I can," "you're right, she's better," I felt the cold steal of the knife cut across my back, I cried out...when he pulled out of me, I fell to the floor, he cleaned himself off of me. Clyde then stuck a needle in my arm, I don't know what he injected into my system but it made me light headed, I kept blacking out. Clyde had placed my clothes on my body, I felt weak, I just laid there on the floor trying to move. "You fucked up," I watched him light a match and drop it on the floor; I started screaming and trying to get up. Clyde stood back, as I watched my family burn, "it didn't have to be this way," he said letting a tear fall from his eye, and then he walked out the house.

11:00am, I woke up in the hospital, I looked around my room, Mya called in a doctor to check me out because I was awake. "Where are my mom and Lily?" Mya looked at me with tears in her eyes, "there gone DJ." I shook my head no, I pulled the IVs out of my arms, pulled myself out of bed and started calling for my mom and sister. "Mom...Lily," I kept sayin over and over again, as tears came down my face, Mya kept yelling for the doctors not to inject me with anything and just take me to see them...I was placed in a wheelchair and taken to the coroner, there bodies laid there burnt like charcoal, I placed my hand on the window, "we were going to watch all dogs go to heaven Christmas carol today, Lily loved that movie," I started hitting the glass with my fist out of anger and sadness until my hand begins to bleed. I looked down and saw blood coming from my side, I pulled my stitches, I slid down the wall, laid my head on my knees and cried. I felt Mya wrap her arms around me, and I fell into her arms like a child, letting the tears fall from my eyes like rain...

Day 137: July 9, 2008

4:38pm, I pace the floors of the bedroom in Mya's house, I kept thinking to myself about how I don't have a home to go to. I went by there and saw it, burned; I found out that one of the neighbors had pulled me out. The fucked up part was that Clyde was no longer a suspect; I found out that he was going to divorce my mom, and that he was already planning on getting married to the woman that he would bring over to the house. To top it off he already had two kids by her who were around me and Lily's age. I had no proof that he was there, I could have told my story a hundred different ways and still not get what I wanted because his whereabouts were proven to be true. I sat on the bed just looking out the window as the light faded into the night, Mya had came into the room and sat behind me, I laid my head back on her shoulder, "you have to try and sleep tonight," "I know." We both got into the bed, I cuddled up in her arms, and I finally went to sleep.

8:00am, I woke up to an empty bed, I turn to see my business suit laid out for me, I got up, took a shower, and got dressed. I stood there looking out the window, it was windy outside, I kissed the ring that was on my thumb and then the necklace around my neck. I put my gloves on my hands, Mya called for me; I put my jacket on and made my way downstairs. We head out the door and make our way to the church. Closed caskets, there pictures sitting beside them, tears came from my eyes, I wish that I was able to control myself for a moment to speak, but all I could get out was "I miss you so much and I love you." After the service we went to the burial ground, I stayed until they lowered the bodies into the ground, Mya stood there right beside me. I wanted to be alone, but we had a repast at the house for friends and some of the family. I stood in the living room, with a glass of water in my hand, just looking out into the backyard. It was going to take some time to accept the fact that they were gone. "DJ there is someone here to see you," said Mya, I turned around only to see my father standing there, his face was full of sadness. "Deavin all I can say is that I am sorry...I should have been there for you," I just stared at him, took a sip of my water and then sat it on the table. "All you can say is sorry? I don't need, nor do I want your apology, I reached out to you five times and you couldn't even call me once, I lost everything," "you didn't lose me," "I lost you the day you left my mother, I called you when I needed you, but I guess you were to busy fucking your new wife and taking care of your new family," "Deavin I..." "Spare the explanation, along with the bullshit...I think, better yet I feel that you should leave this house because you disgrace not only me, but everyone in this house with your presences." He opened his mouth to speak but no words came out, he just turned and walked out the door.

I was relieved to get out of those clothes; I put on sweats and a t-shirt. I held a picture of my mom and sister as I laid in bed, I was finally able to go to sleep on my own. When I woke up the next morning I saw Mya standing there looking at me, "are you hungry?" "Yes." I got out of bed and made my way to the living room where there were pancakes and All Dogs go to Heaven Christmas Carol was on TV. I smiled and sat down to eat and watch it...later that day I walked out on to the patio, Mya was sitting down in the chair, "Mr. Arroyo?" he turned and looked at me, "I just want to say thank you for letting me stay here, and I will never forget your kindness," "Deavin, you can stay here as long as you want. I love you like you were my daughter," "Thank you sir," "call me David you're family now." He hugged me so tight that I couldn't help but to let tears fall from my eyes.

Day 149: July 21, 2008

Many of you now are saying that I have been thru hell, I did and I still was. The death of my family, Clyde not going to jail for there murder, had an affect on me...in June of 2005 I had graduated from high school, I really hated going to my graduation because my mom and sister weren't there to cheer me on, it had already been 8 months since there death, but Mya helped me thru...the next month, on July 20, 2005 marked me and Mya's second year anniversary. I couldn't believe that we had already been together this long. I had started to become a bit more happier, that void was beginning to get filled in by the love of my girl, her father, and new friends that I had made...but as you can see part of me continued to be incomplete, and that feeling lead me to being behind bars. And as I sit behind these walls I couldn't help but to think about how many people sit in jail for years on death row and never get executed. Part of me would wonder at times if I was justified in what I did or should I have just moved on from it. I have come to realize that I am a person that does things based on how I feel, I just wanted to feel better, to feel more alive then what I was feeling...I just didn't realize that prison was going to be the last home that I had ever known.

Day 164: August 5, 2008

June 27, 2006…"Raise and shine," I heard Mya say as she came into my room and opened the curtains, I could feel the sun on my face, and I turned and opened my eyes. "Come on get up DJ, you can't stay in bed on your birthday," "the hell I can, it's my birthday and I can do what I want," "just get out the bed and get ready," she pulled the covers off of me as she walked out the room. I laid there for a few minutes, got out of bed and got ready.

When I walked out the room David had gave me a hug and card for my birthday, he was a good man. I sat down and started eating some French toast; before I knew it Mya was pulling me out the house and into the car. "Don't drop that in my car," I just looked at her and shook my head. Once we got to the mall, I swear we went into every store in there…we stopped at Foot Locker and got me some new white on white Air Forces…we then went to the Levi store and got me some jeans and a nice shirt to wear…I stopped her in front of Victoria Secrets and a big smile went across my face, I took her hand and walked her inside to look at some lingerie. "Go away baby so I can pick out something sexy for you," "I wanna see it," "You will later on tonight," "oh come on," "go DJ or I am walking out of here right now." I walked out the store and started trying on some sunglasses…20 mins later, she walks out of the store smiling. We go to the food court and sit down and eat…as I was taking a bite of my pizza I saw Clyde walking around the mall with his family, Mya turned my face toward her, "don't DJ, not right now," my eyes watered, I put my pizza back down and just sat there…we ended up leaving the mall with the food to go.

Later that night, my party was going on in the house, I just sat in my room on the bed listening to all the noise on the outside. Mya had eventually come into my room; she sat down next to me. "Today you are 18 and all you want to do is sit in your room," "I danced and socialized for a little bit," "you're upset," "I am…my mom and sister died because of Clyde, a man who is on the outside, knowing what he did to them and not given a damn about it," "you're going to kill him aren't you," I just turned and looked at her, "damn it DJ," I stood up "someone has to care, someone has to make it right, and it has to be me," I kneeled down in front of her, "Mya you know I love you more then anything, but this is something that I have to do," "if you loved me, then you wouldn't do this to me." She got up and brushed pass me, I quickly grabbed her hand, stood up, placed my hand on the back of her neck and kissed her as I pushed her back against the wall. "I love you Mya," I ripped open her shirt, letting it drop to the floor as I took off her bra, my hands searched her body as I bit and sucked on her neck, "I love you too," she whispered. I moved her down to the bed, pulled off her pants and thong; I stood there and pulled off my shirt and sports bra, as I laid my body on top of hers. I started kissing and sucking on her neck, i felt her arms wrap around me, as I bit her, I made my way down her body kissing and licking every part of her, sucking on both of her breast as I caressed them. My tongue moved down her stomach and between the lips of her sweet pussy, while I licked and sucked on her like a lollipop, I slowly pushed my fingers inside of her and begin fucking her as I tasted her sweetness. I could feel her nails dig into my back as she moaned and tried to pull away from me; I just locked my arm around one of her legs and kept her at bay. I wanted her to cum for me; I wanted to taste her all over my tongue, she got louder, I went faster and harder. She tasted like a fresh peach on a good day, and when she came the taste only got better. I licked every part of her, as I made my way back up her body. "I should be doing this to you," she said catching her breath, "I wanted to taste you," I started kissing on her neck, "you know we have to get back to the party," "mhm," I continued to kiss her neck and suck on it, "DJ," "I love it when you say my name."

She lifted my head up, got on top of me, and started kissing me. Her hands begin to caress my breast as she licked on me and bit me, fuck I love that, she moved down to my waist, loosened my belt, un buttoned my jeans, un zipped my pants, then pulled them down, her hand slowly moved into my pussy as she felt my wetness, she moved off of me and let her tongue walk all over me, I closed my eyes and continued to feel Mya on my pussy…then she stopped, I sat up and looked at her, "whats wrong?" she stood up "we have to get back to the party," she started getting dressed, I sat there puzzled, "but the party is in here." I got dressed and made my way to the party with Mya, all I could think about was laying her down by the pool and making love to her in front of everyone.

The next day I woke up with a smile on my face, Mya was sleeping peacefully, I looked at the lingerie on the floor, I guess she had a plan all along. I got out the bed and went to the bathroom. I stood there looking at myself in the mirror and began to brush my teeth as Mya came in and did the same. "I am always going to love you DJ, no matter what you do," she said as she sat on the sink on the side of me, "I will too," I moved between her legs and gently kissed her lips, "you know what that means right?" "Nope." She placed her arms around my neck, I put my hands on her hips, then she started to sing, I never heard her do it that much, she sounded so beautiful as she sung Alicia Keys-Like you'll never see me again. I listened to her pour her heart into that song, as I pulled her close to me and held her in my arms. For the first time I knew that this was love, that this was real love, and that no matter what happened between us our hearts would always belong to each other. For the first time I knew in my heart that I wanted to marry her, to make her my wife…I was consumed with so much love in my heart and soul, that the pain cut through it because I knew that if I killed Clyde and his family, I would not be able to look in her eyes anymore or hold her close. I was at a cross road.

Day 174: August 15, 2008

I sit down against the wall in my cell; I started thinking about that day when I truly understood the meaning of real love. The ability to love someone forever and always, even if you were with another person, that's what Mya was. I had to figure out if my love for Mya was stronger then the love that I had for my mom and my sister. Do I just continue to live my life with my girl or do I take the life of the man who killed my family? You would think that this would be the easiest decision in the world to make; you would think that I would just say my family is more important to me then anyone. You also have to remember that this is the first true love that I have ever had. In my heart I loved Mya more then anything, but I knew that I couldn't just sit back and let this man be happy and go on with his life as if he never did anything…it was like part of me knew that I could move on from this and spend the rest of my life with Mya…I even went and got a ring, I made her a promise to my heart and my soul. She still wears it everyday and night. I miss her, I miss her touch, I miss her laugh, I miss hearing her voice, I miss seeing her. I hate that I am locked in this place…

Day 180: August 21, 2008

August 2006, I was already in my third semester of college, I had an English and Cinema class with Mya, along with Biology and Math. Today the professor wanted to have a debate about abortion, now everyone on this earth knows that this is a very touchy subject. I just said "people should have a choice if they want to keep a baby or not, what if you were raped and got pregnant with the guys baby, you might not want to keep him or her," then some girl started going off at the mouth, "no life should be taken just because something happened, for all I know you could of put yourself in that position to get raped because you were tryin to be fast or you wanted to follow the popular kids and do what they do, in got caught up, any girl who kills a kid should be killed them damn selves." I looked over at Mya as the girl continued to talk; something wasn't right with her, the next thing I know she yelled out "shut up," the girl looked at her, "you have no idea what its like to be in that position, until you are in it yourself, you don't know the state of mind of these girls," "I know that any girl who wants to be a slut and have sex just because, she needs to take care of her responsibility," "its not always that easy," "how would know?" the class got quiet when Mya said that she was raped, my jaw dropped open, the professor said "we don't have to talk about this," "I'm comfortable with it now," Mya said, "I was raped by the time I was 16, I ended up getting pregnant. Now I knew that I could have gone and got an abortion because I didn't want the kid to suffer, I didn't want to look at him or her every time and see the man that raped me. I thought about adoption, I knew that he or she would have a good home. I was scared. I decided to have the baby, he was a beautiful baby boy, I held him in my arms and I didn't see the man you raped me, I saw a boy who was going to grow up and break little girls hearts. His name is Elijah, he is now two years old (she looked at me), I kept him and raised him with the help of my family."

When school was over and we went back home, I just sat in the backyard, I couldn't believe that she didn't tell me about him...he is the same age of the time that we had been together. Mya had came and sat down with me, I didn't even look at her. "Before I met you, I had him; I didn't want to tell you anything about him because I felt that you would leave just like everyone else. And when I fell in love with you I knew that I was going to have to tell you," I just sat there looking her, "I know that this wasn't how you should of found out, and I apologize for that." tears came down her face as she made her way back into the house. "You can't be mad at her," said David as he stood in the doorway, "why not? that's not a secret that you keep and then reveal to an entire classroom before you even tell your girlfriend," "Deavin, I have watched my daughter meet all types of women, good, bad, stupid, smart, you name it and I've seen it. When she was raped, she told her then girlfriend, at first she was fine, and then she left her. Every other person just couldn't handle it. When she gave birth, she didn't want to keep him, when she held him, she cried...I let her auntie take care of him, until she was ready to take care of him. And she slowly came around each and every day, until he started comin over more often. Then one day she met you, and she was terrified that if you found out, you would leave because you don't want a girlfriend with a baby." I sat there in silence with tears floating in my eyes, David went

133

back into the house and I followed behind him. I went up to Mya's room and closed the door behind me. "I understand if you don't want to be with me anymore," she said not looking at me, "I couldn't leave you if I wanted to," "why is that?" "Because, I am madly in love with you." I laid down on the bed with her and held her in my arms, "I love you, and we are going to make this work."

Day 182: August 23, 2008

Right now I smile as I write, Elijah is an awesome little boy, and I met him that night after I had found out about him. I was surprised that he knew my name. We started doing things together as if we were a family, we would go to the zoo, park, Disneyland. I loved that little boy and I loved his mother even more. I do remember one thing though, *one day we were all at the mall and I was looking at some shoes to get him, as I waited for the guy to come back, a familiar voice whispered into my ear, I saw Clyde stand right beside me, "it's good to see you Deavin," he said with a smile, "sorry I can't say the same," "don't be that way Deavin, we had fun together," "you ruined my life," "if anything I made your life better, I loved you like you needed to be loved, and I gave you everything that you wanted," "you raped me from the time I was 8 until the day my mom kicked your ass out the house," "I still had my last taste of you, and you know something, I really miss that taste." I turned and faced him, before the words could leave my mouth, his daughter and wife had came over, "honey this is Deavin, she is the daughter of my previous wife, her mother died in a fire along with her daughter Lily, Deavin was the only one to survive," "I am sorry for your lost Deavin, maybe one day you would like to come over for a family dinner," she said to me, "maybe." I turned and walked out of the store leaving what I was there to get.* Wow, that's some crazy shit...I couldn't live knowing that every now in then I would run into him, and he would say shit to get under my skin and piss me off. That moment lead me to a place beyond measures and I didn't care to know what was at the end of the tunnel. All I knew was that I wanted him six feet under; I didn't care if his family went or not, that son of a bitch was most likely hurting those kids as well and they are not saying anything because of fear. I would hate myself to brush him off as someone else's problem because I know that once it comes out he is going to be long gone and having a nice life and family. And on that day I decided that his life will come to an end, and this world will be a little bit better.

I heard Lucky walk pass my door whistling a tune, she always had a musical side to her which I enjoyed. "You come up with a title yet?" said Lucky standing by my door," "yea I did," "what is it?" "In time I will tell you, I promise, I just want to get to a certain point in my story," "I understand…its time for lights out." I put my notebook and pen down, and closed my eyes, "goodnight Lucky," "goodnight DJ."

Day 200: September 10, 2008

December 2006…we are finally free from school for winter recess. I thought that it would never end. School is only fun when you have professors that you wish you could see everyday, not ones that you wish you could press mute on. But I'm not going to work my brain about it, its done, I passed, and now I am moving on. Now when I say moving on, I am talking about Clyde and if I should make him watch his family die or just take him out. *what to do.* I guess that if I am going to do this, then no holds bars, I'm killing them all.

Day 210: September 20, 2008

Lucky had came and got me out of my cell, I followed her down the hallway and into the office. I had finally got a chance to talk to Mya. "Hello," she said, "hey beautiful," "how are you my love?" "I'm hanging in there, how are you and Elijah?" "we're fine, he loves going to school. He misses you. I miss you," "I miss him too and I miss you more," "I love you, always and forever," "I love you too, forever and always." There was a part of me that wanted to tell her to move on when I am gone and don't put your life on hold, but I couldn't get it out. I can admit that part of me was selfish. I believed that it would be hard to tell someone that you are talking to that they were executed for killing someone. This sucks.

Day 226: October 6, 2008

June 2007…I was woken up by Elijah pulling on the covers, I pulled him on the bed with me and tickled him to death. Soon Mya walked in and told us that we had to start getting dress, Elijah left the room and I closed the door. Mya pushed me back onto the bed, "I thought you wanted me to get ready," "I do, and I want to help you." she pulled off her rob and revealed a black matching bra and panties set. I started to pull off some of my clothing as I watched her go into the bathroom and turn on the shower. I walked into the bathroom and kicked the door shut…

4 hours later…we made our way to the mall to hang out and do some shopping, as I stood outside the store waiting for them to come out. I heard a women's voice say my name, I turned around and was face to face with Mary, Clyde's daughter, "I wanted to know if I could talk to you about something," "sure, whats up?" words couldn't seem to come out of her mouth, so I gave her my number and told her to call or text me anytime. "What was that about?" Mya asked standing next to me, "I wish I knew."

Day 240: October 20, 2008

"Hey DJ, you got mail my friend," Lucky said as she handed it to me. I had a letter from Mya, of course, she faithfully writes to me. Raven, that's my homie; I thought she had forgotten about me. And my dad also sent me a letter, which surprised me. I opened his first. He had apologized to me for not being there for me when I needed him most, he said that he felt that it was his fault that they had passed away, and he continued to say that he should have been a better husband to my mother. Tears fell from my eyes to the paper, I could barely control myself. It made me feel overwhelmed that he would even care enough to write to me. I guess some part of him did care about me, but I really didn't know how I felt about him or what to write back to him.

Day 291: December 10, 2008

Today is Mya's birthday; I wish that I could be right there with her celebrating. I would of did whatever it is that she wanted to do, and at the end of the night just hold her in my arms. So Mya, my love, my life, I just want to tell you happy birthday and that I love you more then anything in the world.

Day 306: December 25, 2008

Merry Christmas!! I don't know what else to say. You guys get to open boxes, while I live in one. I can say that one of my favorite Christmas songs is Donell Jones-my gift to you. I hope that you bring in the New Year safely, I'll see you next you year.

Day 328: January 15, 2009

Thanksgiving…8:00am, I woke up feeling amazing. Mya had me up all night last night. I start getting ready for my day. I took the jewelry that my mom and sister had given me and put it in a box, and placed it next to there picture. I then packed myself an overnight bag because I was going to Clyde's house for dinner tonight.

Mya's family started showing up around one, we hugged and greeted each other, and then we all sat down at the table to eat. When it was time for dessert me and Mya had went outside with her strawberry cake. "What are you smiling about?" "you know the first time we had sex was on Thanksgiving," I looked over at her, "and then my dad interrupted," we both started laughing, "I wanted you to taste me so bad that night," "I ended up getting my taste in the end." I held her in my arms. I dug my hand in my pocket and pulled out a locket, "I get this for you," I placed it around her neck,

"I'm always going to be in your heart, even in death." I kissed her on her neck, and pulled her close to me.

4:00pm...I left the house and went to the cemetery to visit my mom and my sister for the last the time. I had placed flowers and a teddy bear on there stones for them...30 minutes later, I was back on the road and driving to Clyde's house. Once I had arrived, I texted Mya to let her know that I was safe.

6:30pm...we all set at the table eating dinner, they tried to make me feel like family as best they could. "So Deavin," said Clyde as he stuck some food in his mouth, "where is that pretty little girlfriend of yours?" "with her family," "how long have you two been together?" "its been 4 years now," "impressive," "I never thought anyone would ever love me," I said coldly, Clyde's expression changed. "Why?" asked Clyde's wife, "because I was always told that I was never going to be loved by anyone, but I seemed to prove them wrong," "I don't see how anyone could say that to someone," "it happens," "well I hope that person who has done you wrong gets whats coming to them, because Karma is a...you know," "I know and he will."

12:30am...I looked at my cell phone, placed it in my pocket and made my way out of the guest bedroom. The family was screaming for help, "no one can hear you," I said as I shook my head. I hit Clyde across the face to wake him up, "what the fuck do you think you're doing?" "Giving you what you deserve," "what I did was out of love," "love? You don't even know what that means." I wheeled his chair out of the house and into the backyard. I went back inside and turned off all the lights. I poured gas all over them and then out the door to Clyde's chair. I lit a match and dropped it. I watched it trail its way into the house, Clyde's face was stone. I started to wonder if he even cared that his family was burning alive. I picked up a crow bar and stood on the side of him, "you know I will always be the best you ever have," "don't you mean had, because for the past 4 years Mya has been the one giving me ultimate satisfaction." I took the end of the crow bar and stabbed him in his manhood; the scream that came out of his mouth couldn't be concealed. I smiled. I started beaten him with the crow bar severely in his face and chest, everything that I was feeling came out. Before I knew it, I was being handcuffed and placed into the back of a police car. I had arrived at the police station covered in blood and a smile on my face.

Day 343: January 30, 2009

We have come to the conclusion that the crimes I have committed were premeditated, I wasn't going to lie and say "it just happened, I didn't know what came over me," I couldn't do that, there is no honor in lying, so I simply said, "I am guilty, I chopped Clyde up and set his family on fire because there was no justice served for the case of my mother and sister."

Day 354: February 10, 2009

I have 20 days left before I get executed; my lawyer is making sure that I am fit for it. I just told him that I am nervous, but I am ready. I think nervous went out the window when he left. I would sit on the floor in my cell, thinking I am scared. I cried more then what I thought I ever would in my life; I even lost myself when I found out what the drugs do to me. you see sodium pentothal is injected to make the prisoner unconscious. Then pancuronium bromide is injected, it terminates my breathing and paralyzes the individual. Finally, potassium chloride is injected to stop the heart. Damn. That's something huh…I think I am getting a little depressed. I am just going to lay down and try to gather what thoughts I have left and write letters to my family and friends.

Day 360: February 16, 2009

I got moved to a different security area because my execution order has been received, I get checked on hourly as well because they want to keep track of my behavior. I have no reason to kill myself because they are going to do that for me. I am damn sure not going to lose my mind because while I don't want to go to the crazy house…I cant speak for everyone else who is in this position, but I do know that there is not much to think when you know that in 14 days you are going to die…I feel like I can't even feel my heart beat anymore.

Day 370: February 26, 2009

I cant believe that I have been in jail now for one year and five days, I guess this is what people mean when they say do the time, don't let the time do you. In my case I have spent my time reflecting about my life and making friends, so it wasn't that bad of an experience. I guess that when they let me talk to the Chaplin, I will reveal something that I have kept in all this time. Even in death we have secrets, but I am not going to die with this one. People have the right to know the truth, why? Because the truth shall set you free. In my case it was more of a sacrifice in order for people to live and move on.

Day 374: March 1, 2009

It's the day before my execution, I was moved into a death watch cell which is adjacent to the execution chamber, and there are three members of the staff that watch me. Now what I want to know is how do the expect me to sleep at night knowing that tomorrow I am going to be strapped to a table in the chamber that is not that far from me. I just laid here on my bed and continued writing because sleeping was the last thing on my mind. Trust me I tried about five times, and still didn't get the much sleep. My time is almost up and I am sad as fuck.

Day 375: March 2, 2009- Last 24 hours

The last meal I decided to have was soul food and some strawberry cake. While I sat there the chaplain had came to visit me, I just stared at him for the first few minutes in silence. "I have a confession to make," I said to him, "what would that be?" "I want to go back to the night of the murder," "ok," "and this stays between me and you?" "Yes," "*I had asked the family if they wanted anything to drink, they had conveniently said yes. So in each one of there drinks, I drugged them, so that they would pass out. I tied each of them up to a chair and waited for them to wake up. Once I let Clyde see his family, I rolled him out, when I went back into the house and turned off all the lights, I untied the two sisters. Once I was back outside I lit the match, I told them to get out the house,*" "Why would you do that?" "Because Clyde did to them what he did to me and my sister, and they reminded me of myself and Lily. They were around the same age as we were, and there was no way I could make them pay when there father did the same thing to them." Tears filled my eyes, "*the day of my trail I saw them sitting in the court room, they smiled at me and I smiled back…they came to visit me twice…and they both thanked me for getting rid of him,*" "why didn't you say something?" "I wasn't planning on letting anyone go, I was going to kill them all, and make them suffer. I only did it because I received a text from Mary asking me if Clyde had ever done anything to me, I told her yes, she said me too. I told her she didn't have to say anymore. I freed her in away that I couldn't be freed."

The Chaplain left the room, and I sat there getting myself together. A smile came across my face when I saw Mya walk into the room, I hugged her so tight, and I kissed her and kissed her some more. I sat down and she sat on my lap. While feeding me some cake, David had came into the room and so did my dad. I could honestly say that this is the most emotional night of my life. "You know I don't want you there," I said to Mya, "why not?" "Because I don't want you to watch me die," "DJ, I can handle it, and I want to be the last face that you see when you close your eyes." She gently kissed my lips.

A guard walked in with a pair of denim trousers and a blue work shirt to wear, for the last and final time Mya helped me undress and put on the clothes that I would be executed in. I hugged each and every one of them. I held Mya the longest; I felt her tears on my shirt, as I tried to control myself. I gave her the longest kiss that I could give her. We parted ways and I was taken to the execution chamber, and strapped to the table. I was then connected to a cardiac monitor, and an IV was started in two usable veins. A normal saline solution was given to me at a slow rate. The door was then closed. I was able to see the witnesses. I spotted Lucky standing behind the people; she pounded her chest and pointed to the sky. Tears came down my cheek as I stared into Mya's eyes and mouthed "I love you always and forever," "I love you forever and always." The warden issued the execution order.

The End

Thank You:

I would like to say thank you to everyone who has and continues to support me in this journey of becoming a writer. My dream is to continue writing books, that will capture your attention and your heart.

If you would like to get in contact with me please feel free to email me at elwalker101@gmail.com.